UN.ORTHODOX

SARAH,

KEEP SERVING CHRIST!

+ URBAN D.

Un.orthodox

church • hip-hop • culture

Tommy Kyllonen

aka Urban D.

ZONDERVAN®

ZONDERVAN.com/
AUTHORTRACKER
follow your favorite authors

We want to hear from you. Please send your comments about this
book to us in care of zreview@zondervan.com. Thank you.

Un.orthodox
Copyright © 2007 by Tommy Kyllonen

Requests for information should be addressed to:

Zondervan, *Grand Rapids, Michigan* 49530

Library of Congress Cataloging-in-Publication Data
  Kyllonen, Tommy, 1973 –
    Un.orthodox : church, hip-hop, culture / Tommy Kyllonen aka Urban D.
      p. cm.
    Includes bibliographical references.
    ISBN-13: 978-0-310-27439-1
    ISBN-10: 0-310-27439-7
      1. City churches—United States.   2. Crossover Community Church (Tampa, Fla.)
    3. Kyllonen, Tommy, 1973 –   4. Hip-hop.   5. Church work with youth—United States.
    6. Urban youth—Religious life—United States.   I. Title.   II. Title: Unorthodox.
    BV637.K95 2007
    253 — dc22   2006100427

Interior design by Nancy Wilson

Printed in the United States of America

07 08 09 10 11 12 13 14 • 22 21 20 19 18 17 16 15 14 13 12 11 10 9 8 7 6 5 4 3 2 1

Contents

PART ONE

An Unorthodox Life
My Story

PART TWO

An Unorthodox Culture
Hip-Hop's History

PART THREE

An Unorthodox Approach
Ministry to the Culture

Shout-Outs

To my family—from my grandparents down to my parents—who followed God's calling and became unorthodox: the lives you modeled helped shape mine. Dad, your leadership, your compassion, and your love for people and for your family flow through my veins. Ma, I'm proud of you! You've been so strong through everything that's happened over the years, especially the past six. We got your back! *S' Agapo Puli!* Tammy, you'll always be my lil' sis who loves to sing and loves to give gifts. Keep giving those gifts to the world. Lucy, my soul mate, my ministry partner, my babies' mamma! I wouldn't be who I am today without you. Our best years are still to come. *Te amo, mi amor.* Papi's girls (my daughters), Deyana Luz and Sophia Alexia—you both always put a smile on my face and make everything seem a lot brighter. To the rest of my family—the Laguerras, the Kyllonens, the Givas—thank you for all your love and support over the years.

My Crossover family, a few of you have been around for nearly a decade, but most of you have joined this exciting journey during the past couple of years. Thank you for being innovators and being willing to change as we continue to grow this unique faith community with a New Testament flavor in a hip-hop context. This is "our" church! You all inspired much of the last few chapters of this book. Big shout-outs to all the ministry leaders, volunteers, and staff who serve our community with their time and energy. Spec, I thank you for your countless sacrifices since our humble beginnings. You've not only poured into many lives, your creativity has visually helped us become the model we are. Tone, I thank you for your leadership, your council, and your friendship over the decades since the time we were aimless in the streets of Philly. It's crazy what God has done. Josie, God has incredibly used you to create an authentic hip-hop/R&B worship experience that ushers our culture into his presence. *Gracias* for your faithfulness. Gordon, for never giving up on what God said he was going to do! Derrick, big ups for joining our team and reshaping our Third Rail teen ministry. Till the culture knows!

Much love to those who have mentored me through this journey these past few years: Dave Holden, Joe McCutchen, Jeff Yale, Mark Rutland, Mike Estep, Mark Beeson, Rick Warren, and several other PD pastors.

Big thanks to all the ministries across the country that I've partnered with over the years. To all my fellow pastors, youth pastors, and church leaders impacting the culture—this is just the beginning! To all my fellow artists reppin' Christ on the mic—keep spittin' the uncompromised truth to the masses. Special thanks goes out to Jeff Lambert for believing in this project and paving the way. Angela, Jamie, Rob, Brian, and the rest of the team at Zondervan: thank you guys for seeing the need, recognizing the movement, and getting behind it.

Introduction

I love the church. I love hip-hop. These two statements make sense on their own, but when you put them together, the combination seems unorthodox. To many it may even sound like an oxymoron. It may put some real concern in a church leader's or a parent's heart. Church and hip-hop? How could those two ever go together? I understand that question, and I don't blame you for asking. Sometimes I feel like we don't ask enough questions. This book isn't about some guy who grew up loving hip-hop and tried to fit it into church because he didn't want to let it go. When I got fully committed to Christ in my late teens, I was ready to let it all go. I thought I needed to walk away from it and become like everyone else in my church. But God showed me I wasn't supposed to be like everyone else. As I fell in love with Christ and his church, I noticed how many of my peers weren't seeing or feeling what I was experiencing with my creator. God soon made it clear I was called to be an indigenous missionary to my culture. But what would that look like?

This culture that captivated me in elementary school in the early eighties has now become a global multi-billion-dollar industry. Thirty years after its beginning, its influence has crossed all geographical, economic, and racial barriers. It reaches well beyond the teen and college demographics. The majority of urban music (hip-hop and R&B) is now bought by white people from the suburbs. But hip-hop is not just a music genre; it's a lifestyle encompassing attitude, fashion, and worldview.

I always try to put myself in other people's shoes. I know I'm called to bridge gaps and to translate to different people groups. Sometimes it's to people in the culture as I break down the faith. Sometimes it's to people in the faith as I break down the culture. Clearly much of the message of today's mainstream hip-hop is pretty negative. If you're on the outside looking in, this negativity seems even more magnified. Headline news over the years has featured rappers killed in drive-by shootings, organizations trying to censor the violence and profanity in rappers' lyrics, shootings at concerts and clubs, and on and on. Adding to the stereotype, when you go to the mall, you see groups of teens and younger adults in baggy clothes staring you down with intimidating looks. You pull up to a stoplight and the car next to you is blasting some rap music. Your vehicle shakes and every other word needs to be bleeped out. This may be the only side you see. It seems angry, scary, and out of control. You may wonder how anything good could come out of something so negative. So I understand the initial question.

But most people—even most people who would consider themselves hip-hoppers—don't really know the details of how this culture started. Most people's perception is based on what they see on MTV, BET, and VH1. It's based on what they hear on Top 40 radio, what they read in magazines like *The Source* and *XXL*, and the sites they come across on MySpace and the rest of the net.

We can all agree that hip-hop is in serious need of a spiritual reformation. But to bring reformation, we must understand hip-hop's current form and how it got there. Several chapters of this book take an in-depth look at the history, the demise, and the current state of the culture. Some who claim Christ will make ignorant statements that hip-hop is from the devil. They'll twist the history and say it even started as a false religion. They'll even go so far as to say it's unredeemable. Those without cultural and biblical knowledge will jump on these bandwagons. It's an easy way for them to stick to their preferences and not engage with people who are different from them.

But when we look at Scripture, the people of God were all about engaging cultures that weren't in a relationship with him. Jonah got called to Nineveh, Philip ministered to and baptized an Ethiopian, and Paul got called to the Gentiles. Just outside our windows is a whole mission field full of hip-hop-influenced youth and adults who are without a relationship with Christ. Statistics show that the church in the United States is on the verge of losing the majority of the next generation. Many say we're entering a post-Christian era. This is a crisis!

Sure, aspects of hip-hop culture can't be used for godly purposes, but several neutral aspects of the culture can give us a platform to present truth. Again, I'll stress that hip-hop is not just music; it's also dance, art, poetry, film, style, and much more. These things can be used as vehicles to engage people and to communicate and illustrate the gospel and its worldview. The Roman Empire ruled during the early days of the church. Although the empire created many obstacles for Christ-followers, it also created a road system that helped spread the word. Hip-hop can be looked at as today's Roman roads. It is a pipeline to younger generations of all ethnic groups across the planet. It creates an opportunity for us to spread the message of Jesus Christ.

Un.orthodox is a resource to help you navigate today's culture and see that it is reachable. This book shares some of my story, some of hip-hop's story, and some of Crossover Community Church's story, all stories which are highlighted by Christ's story and what can happen when he gets in the picture. I pray that you'll be encouraged by and excited about what Christ is doing in culture through his church. The church must be the missionary agent that carries the message of Christ to the culture. I love the church, and I love hip-hop, but even more I love Jesus Christ, and I love when people from my culture and all cultures get redeemed by him!

PART ONE

church • hip-hop • culture

An Unorthodox Life

My Story

1

PK
(Philly Kid)

Being unorthodox is in my blood, passed down through generations of men and women who lived out-of-the-ordinary lives. My own life as a rebellious preacher's kid hooked on hip-hop is itself unorthodox. Yet in my heritage and in my life, being unorthodox was clearly part of the plan.

My unorthodox roots begin in Greece with my grandfather on my mother's side. Efthimios Demetios Givas was from a small struggling village in Greece. He didn't come to America in 1921 for democracy or religious freedom. He came because he was hungry. He heard there was lots of food in America, and he was tired of wondering where his next meal was coming from. After many years of barely getting by, my grandfather became a cook on a shipping vessel that made trips across the Atlantic. When the ship was anchored in Boston Harbor, my grandfather and two other Greek guys jumped into the frigid waters in the middle of the night and swam for shore. Even though he was a strong swimmer, having grown up on the Mediterranean, he nearly drowned that night as the cold water cramped his muscles. After wandering around the city for days, they finally connected with the Greek community. Some Greeks helped my grandfather get to New Jersey, where he had some family. He landed a job at a restaurant and eventually became an incredible assistant chef at the Essex House in Newark—the largest and classiest hotel in New Jersey. In 1933, a special law was passed to allow illegal immigrants to get citizenship if they had arrived in America before 1925. He waited in line for two days to become a legal citizen.

Even though my grandfather experienced culinary success and obtained U.S. citizenship, gambling took hold of his life for several years as a young man. Seeing his destructive ways, his cousin, who was a Christian, urgently dragged him to a church service on West 36th Street in Manhattan. It was different from anything my grandfather had ever experienced. He soon built an authentic relationship with Christ and did the unthinkable: he left the Greek Orthodox Church, which he had grown up in, and became a faithful member of this Christian Greek community. Church soon became his favorite place to be. Because he had left the Greek Orthodox Church, he was ostracized from Greek society. But my grandfather didn't care. He became unorthodox. Suddenly, everything was new, everything was fresh. His decision would forever determine the direction of my family and the direction of my life.

Roots Chapter 3

66 Crystal-clear water, white sands ■ exotic tans ■ my ethnic roots trace back to these types of foreign lands ■ but it wasn't in his plans ■ for this ill format

Unorthodox roots took hold on the other side of my family too. Anti (Andrew) Kyllonen was my grandfather on my father's side. His parents arrived in America from Finland a few years before he was born and settled in the Pittsburgh area, where his father worked at a tin mill. As immigrants, my great-grandparents held strong to the language and traditions of the old country. They sometimes attended the Finnish Lutheran Church in their community. For many, the church represented a culture and community rather than a place for spiritual experiences. Even though my grandfather went through confirmation at age fifteen, it really wasn't personal or real to him.

As Anti got older, he searched for meaning and purpose in his life. On June 20, 1930, he sat on the Finnish Club Bench and heard about a church service that night. He decided to go. When he walked into the church, there were only three people there, including him. But the man preaching spoke as passionately as if the room were packed with people. That night, my grandfather accepted Christ. Soon after, he got baptized, even though several Finnish people told him he didn't need to do that since he had been baptized as a child. But he knew God was doing something in him. Everything became new, exciting, and real. He broke away from tradition and religion and built a true relationship with his creator. Just like my other grandfather, Anti became unorthodox.

As a result of both of my grandfathers' conversions to Christianity, my parents were the first generations of their families to grow up in true Christian homes. They learned about Christ from young ages, which impacted my life and created an environment that otherwise would have been much different. While in his early twenties, my father chased dead-end jobs and gambling. But God reminded my father that he had called him to the ministry many years before. So he started the journey. One summer at a Christian campground in eastern Pennsylvania, he met a fast-talking girl from New Jersey. My mother was barely five feet tall, and my father, 6' 4½", towered over her. With the difference in height, they were definitely an unorthodox couple. Yet they began a long-distance relationship while he attended Bible college in Rhode Island.

Mi familia immigrated to the urban habitats ▪ sportin' gloves and winter hats ▪ break dancin' on vinyl mats ▪ when it came to ball—using sticks instead of bats ▪ writing raps

A NEW FAMILIA (BIRTH OF A PK)

Three years later, Paul and Elizabeth Kyllonen married and soon moved to western Pennsylvania to pastor their first church. Three years after that, I came along. Thomas, the firstborn preacher's kid that everyone called Tommy.

At the time, my father pastored a tiny church in a small town called Bessemer. This booming metropolis had just over a thousand residents, and everything was centered on the cement plant, which was known to have mafia ties. It was an interesting time for my twentysomething parents, pastoring a church mostly of older attendees and many crazy small-town characters. Back in those days, most pastors didn't usually stay in one church for an extended period of time.

When I was three years old, my family moved to the Allentown area in eastern Pennsylvania. A year later, my sister, Tammy, was born. Some of my childhood memories kick in here. I went to kindergarten. I learned to ride my bike. I learned how to get the church board really upset.

Our house was connected to the church. You could actually walk through a door next to our bedrooms and find yourself in the back of the main auditorium of the church. As I think back now, that seems kind of weird, but it reinforced my feelings of being at home in the church. So I acted like I was at home. Many days after school I would walk over to the church and grab the drumsticks and have a great time making a racket as I banged on the drums. I would explore the church and go downstairs into all the classrooms and even see if there was anything good in the refrigerator in the church kitchen.

One Sunday night after a communion service, I led a group of four or five kids up to the front of the auditorium. All the parents were in the back talking and catching up. Kids always love snacks, and we were all hungry. I had noticed that there were still several cups of that purple juice left in the big silver dish with all the cup holders, along with lots of those cool little wafers. During the service, people get to have only one of each. I could never understand that, because it never filled you up. The Lord's Supper was really small portions. So there we were, looking at all the leftovers. We figured why throw them out when we could finish them off? Service is over and nobody will notice. Why waste it? Well, when I drank the purple juice, the others followed, just in time for one of the stuffy board members

Graffiti covered landscapes ▪ Philly cheese steaks ▪ pounds and shakes ▪ with cons and fakes ▪ for goodness' sakes

to catch us in the act. I thought it was no big deal, but I noticed that some of the adults got pretty upset. Later that night when I walked through the door connecting the church to our house, my parents were pretty upset at me as well. I explained that I was really hungry and that I was a growing boy. My protests didn't get me too far. The church board actually called my father for an official meeting about the "communion incident."

Shortly after, my family made another move, not because of my after-service behavior but because of the constant drama many traditionally structured churches tend to have. My father tried to leave the church for over a year. Yet it seemed as if no other doors opened up, except for a church in Philadelphia. At first, he didn't even entertain the idea. My pops wasn't really crazy about raising his young family in a big-city environment. He debated submitting his resume, but the denomination continually reminded him that this church was the only thing available. Then he got a call for an interview from the church leaders at Northeast Assembly of God in Philadelphia. We jumped in our big old Delta 88 Oldsmobile boat and headed down to the city. As we drove down I-95 and entered the city, we looked across the endless horizon of the rooftops of row homes. I remember asking my mom why all the houses were stuck together and looked exactly alike.

THE BIG MOVE

One of my father's major concerns was where we would live. While my mother had experienced life as a city girl in northern New Jersey, my pops only knew life in a small town, growing up just outside of Pittsburgh. He wondered if he could really connect in an urban environment.

As we drove down Frankford Avenue, I was intrigued by the electric city buses connected to the wires above the streets. Everywhere I looked, I saw buildings, people, and graffiti tags. I remember when I

> We knew poverty like a bank account with all zeros ■ eating baklava and gyros ■ dope MCs were my heroes

first saw the church. It was about forty feet wide and two stories high and was positioned between two houses. I asked my mom, "Why is the church squished in?" Even to a six-year-old kid, it seemed like a strange place to put a church. Located on a city block with row homes all around, it had no parking lot. Everyone fought for parking spaces on the surrounding streets, especially on Sundays.

As my parents sat in the interview, my sister and I camped out in the nursery. Of course I had to scope the place out. So I ventured out to see what we were working with. That's what PKs do. All in all, the meeting with the church board went well. They shared that they owned a house for the pastor nine miles north of the church. We weren't able to go see it, so we really didn't know what the house and the area were like. Later that night, our family jumped in our boat of a car and drove back to Allentown. Days later, my father got a call from the leaders at Northeast. They wanted him to candidate—church lingo meaning they wanted him to come and speak at a service to see if the church liked my dad and if we liked them. A few weeks later, we headed back to the City of Brotherly Love.

That Sunday morning, we walked in for Sunday school—only seventeen people and no kids. Quite depressing. In the morning service, there were about fifty people, mostly older and traditional. My father preached and my mother sang. It seemed like everything was cool. After service, we ate some good food at a restaurant and then checked out the church's house, aka the parsonage. During the twenty-minute ride, the scenery began to change. More trees and fewer row homes. The house was on a street with other single-family homes with small yards. A drugstore stood on the corner three houses up, with a grocery store on the other side. My parents were excited when they discovered that the house had a yard that their kids could play in. The house was small but had potential. There was one small bathroom and two bedrooms, as well as two other rooms up in the attic, which were eventually made into bedrooms. My parents breathed a sigh of relief, since everything seemed right for their family. That night, the church members voted unanimously for Paul Kyllonen to be their new pastor.

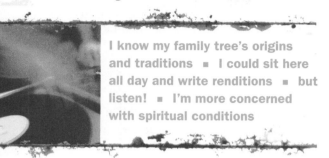

I know my family tree's origins and traditions ▪ I could sit here all day and write renditions ▪ but listen! ▪ I'm more concerned with spiritual conditions

Meanwhile, things got worse at the church in Allentown. No other doors opened. All signs pointed toward Philly. My father accepted the position, and within weeks we packed everything into a big moving truck. A new house, a new neighborhood, a new church, and a new school. It was December 1979, and I was in the first grade. Hip-hop's first hit, *Rapper's Delight*, was brewing in the Bronx. And a major snowstorm hit the East Coast as I headed to my first day at Struble Elementary School. It was a new time. No longer a PK from a small town, I was a new PK— officially a Philly kid.

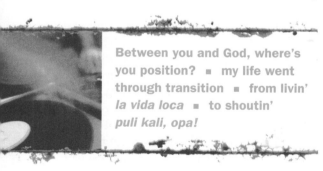

Between you and God, where's you position? ▪ my life went through transition ▪ from livin' *la vida loca* ▪ to shoutin' *puli kali, opa!*

HOMEMADE ITALIAN FOOD

Being a preacher's kid wasn't always an easy thing. Yes, it had its perks. I got extra gifts for my birthday and for Christmas. Our family got invited to people's homes. You didn't expect to eat out that often when your dad was the pastor of a small urban church. But we ate out quite often, because many people took us out and insisted on taking care of the bill. It bothered my father sometimes, but for many people, it was their way of expressing thanks. Our church in Philly was multicultural. Some of the people were first-generation immigrants. Nearly half of the church was Italian, some of whom were actually born in Sicily. Needless to say, I grew up eating a lot of incredible homemade Italian food. We loved to go to the Beneddettos' house, the Philaminas', the Brunos', Sister Lena's, and many others. Great authentic food was definitely a highlight of being a PK.

As I grew up, I noticed that I got special attention. It was great at times. But at other times, it was really a drag because people expected me to always be an angel. They expected me to be the example for all the other kids at the church. I always took charge as a leader, but I didn't lead others the right way. I had a mischievous side. Many times, I crawled under the pews during the service or rolled a ball to my friend, who sat three rows behind me. I became pretty slick and almost went undetected. But when you're at church three and four services a week, you will get caught. Some of my most embarrassing memories are of times when my father stopped his sermon to call me out in front of everyone when I acted up. All the older mem-

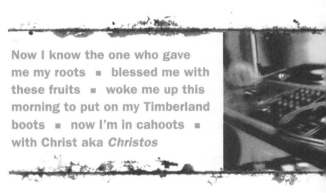

Now I know the one who gave me my roots ■ blessed me with these fruits ■ woke me up this morning to put on my Timberland boots ■ now I'm in cahoots ■ with Christ aka *Christos*

bers after service said things like, "Tommy, you better respect your father and listen during church." As I grew up, I learned to play the game. You know, say the right things and do the right things at the right times.

THE ORTHODOX SYSTEM

As a PK, I saw what happens behind the scenes at churches. Some of it was pretty ugly. The church had the traditional system in which the church board basically ran everything. They controlled the church, and it was very political. Their philosophy was that they had always run it and they always would. Pastors would come and go, but they would be there until they died. I admire their commitment since I don't see it often in today's younger generations. But many times, the control issue got out of balance. Several board members had histories at the church. Many of them were retired and were pillars of the congregation. The church really became their lives. My father, being a younger pastor in his thirties, wanted to make some changes to help the church to grow and be more effective. You would think a small church would want to grow and reach its community. Well, they said they did. But when it came to making some of the changes, it seemed like my father hit a brick wall.

> Steadily studying the Scriptures from the *logos* ■ take it from Efthemios ■ whom he's given madd styles like computer fonts ■ now me and Christ go together like Greeks and restaurants

For example, music is one of the biggest things that determines who will be attracted to your church. My father incorporated a team of singers, a few instruments (besides the piano and organ), and the incredible new technology of the overhead projector. They began singing some new choruses, which was very progressive for the eighties. It caused quite a rumble with the older members of the church, because they preferred hymns exclusively. Even the color that rooms were repainted was a big deal. When the church finally agreed to break down and get rid of the 1960s bright red carpet, some of the younger members put the pews back in on a slight slant to make the church look a little more modern. We all thought it was cool — for pews. But some of the older members were upset and quickly changed them back before they were permanently bolted down. They did end up getting bolted down on a slant, but the funny thing is that when I went back to visit a few years ago, they were back to straight again. Things hadn't changed much.

One of the hardest things to change was the "holy" communion table.

> Rockin' the trilingual flow ■ come here yo ■ *venga aqui* ■ *ellathough* ■ *sash-ef-hotty-stoh* ■ no need for *parakalos* ■ now I'm sportin' Christ's name like some Ecko cargos

The church had an altar rail along the area in front of the stage. There was a big communion table that you could barely walk past if you were behind the altar. Sometimes at the end of a service, my father and some of the other leaders stood behind the altar and would pray for people in front of it. But there was no space to pray. One of the church members, a carpenter, had a great idea. He took the table home and modified the back legs. He resurfaced it and made it look really nice. When he put the table in, everyone appreciated the nice improvement. It created plenty of space behind the altar for the leaders to pray with people. All was good until the oldest board member saw that the two back legs were shorter and rested on the front edge of the stage. This guy was outraged that someone had dared to cut the "holy" communion table's legs! It caused quite an uproar with all the older people that he influenced. Instead of worrying about people's needs, this whole group of people focused on a simple table that was only a tradition, not a biblical necessity.

I watched my father wisely use the art of compromise. He got the carpenter to cut the table's width in half and put on two new legs so they rested on the floor. The new and improved table was now more narrow, allowing people to walk in front of it, and it still had all four legs. The drama of the old orthodox structure system had reared its ugly head, but fortunately in the end everyone was happy.

AUTHENTIC MINISTRY

We lived in Philly for over ten years—the majority of my school-age and teen years. I had the privilege of watching a small dying church of about fifty older people grow to a thriving younger church of close to two hundred. The older outdated building was remodeled with new paint, carpet, equipment, a kitchen, and several upstairs classrooms. It was always under some transformation, constantly progressing and growing.

Reminiscing about those days, I remember all the great things my parents did for people. My pops had the true heart of a pastor. In his early days in Philly, he was still a little naive at times. Con artists, street hustlers, homeless people, and even other pastors took advantage of his loving heart. I remember several different people who stayed at our house when they had nowhere else to go. When I was a young kid, I even gave up my bed a couple of times for some rough characters. God always protected us, and my dad was a pretty big dude, so there were never any safety issues. And the longer my father stayed in Philly, the more his street smarts grew. Yet through it all, he always loved people. He was a very relational dude. Pastor Paul Kyllonen always made his rounds every week, visiting and praying with older people and shut-ins from church.

Authentic ministry happened as strong relationships were built. People's lives changed forever as they got to know Christ and discovered a

Why? cuz he died for you and me ■ now I know my future and my history ■ Urban D. ■ say *s'agapo puli!* 🙌

real community with a real leader. My father's ministry didn't look anything like the ministry I have today. But it was still unorthodox, and it was a breath of fresh air. It's been many years since we left Philly, but my family is still close to many people there, as they have become our extended family—for life and beyond.

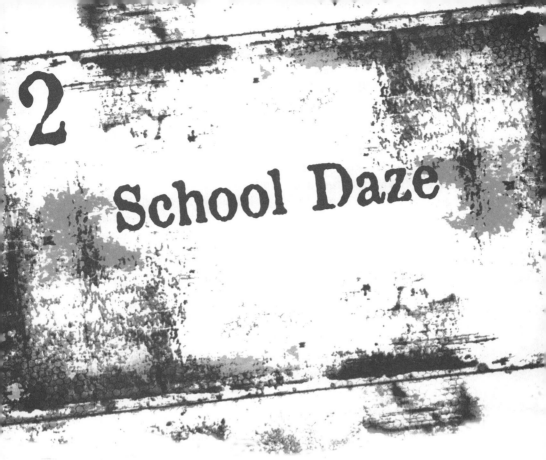

2 School Daze

When I enrolled in my new elementary school as a first-grader, I had to be initiated. A good fight always broke in the new kids. Several kids messed with me on the bus on the way home, and I wasn't having it. I stood up for myself and wouldn't back down even when a dark-skinned dude hit me in the face with his lunch box. But when I felt the pain and saw the blood flow from my nose, I quickly sat down. Just at that moment, the bus came to my stop. Here comes the new kid, little Tommy, getting off the bus crying with a bloody nose. My mom was waiting at the stop. She walked me home and I knew she would fix everything. She called the school the next day to complain, but nothing ever happened. After that day, I soon became cool with the bad kids on the bus and became part of the crew. Although I loved my new school and my new teacher, I found myself in trouble for picking fights with other kids.

Elementary school proved to be an interesting place. It was a new school with funky modern architecture: everything was on one floor, but there were virtually no windows. Each grade had one large room with dividers between four classrooms. Many times, we heard the teacher yelling at her class right next to the half-wall divider. Fifty percent of the kids came from average working-class families. Another quarter came from middle- to upper-class Jewish families, and the remainder from low-income homes. I gravitated toward the low-income kids. Even though my family wasn't as bad off as some of the other low-income kids, I found most of my other classmates stuck up and boring. At lunchtime, I had the revelation that I wasn't like everyone else. Because my family didn't make as much money, we were eligible for the free-lunch program. You know my mom took advantage of that! I didn't care. I thought it was actually cool that I had this piece of paper that got me lunch for free while most of the other kids had to pay. Soon I realized most of my friends also had the tickets as we sat together at the same lunch tables. These kids were the characters. Most of my friends were from broken homes and had a lot of drama going on in their families. Even at a young age I realized how good I really had it.

Skintone

&& The problem's more than skin deep, it's getting down to the bone ▪ when it comes to this country's issues of skintone ▪ *mi Corazon* is broken

All of the kids my age lived on the next block by the bus stop. Our bus stopped in front of a big two-story abandoned building. Trees and weeds grew all around it, and a tall fence with barbed wire surrounded the perimeter. A lot of teens climbed the fence and broke inside to have parties, drink, and get high. On the front of the building, somebody tagged up a big graffiti piece that said "Guzzlers" with a big mug of beer sprayed up next to it. That building became a landmark spot in our hood. I remember telling my mom, "Hey, I'm heading up to Guzzlers to catch the bus." Of course, she never let me go up there alone, because a rough crowd hung out on the corner, and inside and around the building.

MY FIRST PAIR OF NIKES

While my elementary years were fairly uneventful, fifth grade was a turning point. Suddenly I began to look at everyone differently because of my new love: sneakers! Back in those days, peer pressure set in much earlier in metropolitan areas. And while everyone in my crew sported Nikes, my parents were buying my clothes at a thrift store. Although most of it was decent, the sneakers didn't have names. Well, actually they did. The slang on the street for no-name sneakers was Bo-Bo's. They had a song: "Bo-Bo's, they make your feet feel fine; Bo-Bo's, they cost a nickel or a dime." Soon I was getting dogged out by everyone in my class about my kicks, especially since everyone else was rocking Nike and Adidas. When I got home, I begged my mom to take me to the mall to buy me some Nikes. We went to a shoe store and found some low-top suede Nikes for twenty-five dollars. My father said, "Twenty-five dollars?! I'll get you the same ones at K-Mart for seven ninety-nine." Well, I wasn't going out wearing no K-Tracks. Big boy Sammy got teased and pushed around at recess every day for wearing a pair of those. But my pops refused to pay. It was a crucial moment in my life: realizing that in this world nothing with a brand name would be handed over for free. So at ten years old, I went on a mission. I strolled through the neighborhood and pulled weeds, cut grass, and washed cars. Whatever I could do to hustle up some money for my new sneaks. Funny how a simple pair of shoes created a strong work ethic in me. Looking back, I wouldn't trade them because of the lasting things that they instilled in my character. My motives were off balance at times, but it was the start of a foundation that God would later build on.

See where I grew up racial slurs were rarely spoken ■ and if they was, most people was just jokin' ■ we was all in the same boat, strugglin' to get change for a bus token

I raised the money for my shoes within two weeks and headed to the mall for my first coveted pair of Nikes. They were burgundy suede with a gray swoosh. I bought some fat gray laces (we called them New Yorkers) to match the swoosh. I laced them in the uptown style—laces going to the outside were always on top of the ones facing the inside. When I walked into the school, I felt like a million bucks. Everybody noticed my new sneakers! I loved the attention, and I realized that sneakers brought respect in the city. Of course, they also could attract unwanted attention.

CARDBOARD, BOOM BOXES, AND BREAK DANCING

Some of the kids at my church went to much rougher inner-city schools, and they were always a little bit ahead on the trends. I had heard about break dancing, but the first time I actually saw it was, of all places, at church. After service, some of the middle-school and high-school kids hung out upstairs and cleared out all the tables and chairs to begin a session. Joe McGrodery broke out a boom box playing Herbie Hancock and started breaking down some moves. First, he taught us to up-rock as we danced from side to side to the beat. Then we watched in amazement as he got down on the floor and did some moves, topping it all off with a back spin. Break dancing became my second love. I cleared the wood floor in my bedroom and practiced my back spins. Within days, the breaking phenomenon spread to my school and everyone was trying to do it. I actually had one of the best back spins around, so everyone was always asking me to show it off.

Soon, people were breaking everywhere—during class, in the halls, at recess. Our gym teacher actually gave us five minutes to break dance at the beginning of class on the beautiful smooth gym floor (as long as we promised not to break during the rest of class). Many of the popular kids who were breakers wore sweat suits so they could get better spins on the floor. Every recess, about fifty of us gathered around pieces of cardboard that we brought to school to spin on and showed our moves. The biggest and toughest kids in the school always let me in the circle to show off my back spin and my windmills.

Church also became a much more exciting place. After every service, all the youth headed upstairs to the tile floor to show off the latest moves we learned in the different schools we attended. We had our minibattles going on as we competed against each other. Around this same time, Michael Jackson's "Thriller" video came out, which was full of some really cool dancing. At school, if we were good throughout the day, our homeroom teacher, Mr. Kline, showed us the video before we headed out to the bus.

As the dance fad grew out of control, word got out in the media that some people got hurt; some well-known breakers actually broke their necks. Fearing a possible lawsuit, the principal banned it. Some of our parents complained, but the rule remained and our breaking went underground. At the time, I didn't even know this growing movement was called hip-hop. All I knew was that I loved the music, the dress, and the dance, and I was right in the middle of it!

ARMSTRONG MIDDLE SCHOOL

Going to middle school seemed like going off to the real world. It was a lot different from my elementary school, where there were just four classes per grade with everyone in one big room. It was a large, old traditional school building with ten classes per grade, separate classrooms for each period, bells that rang, and lockers in all the halls. It was the real deal. The crowd was more urban and more diverse. Each sixth-grade class had a number next to it according to the students' academic ability. The number 6-1 was the "smartest" class, and 6-10 was the "not so smart" class. I was in the 6-3 class, so that wasn't so bad. Most of my elementary school crew were in the higher-numbered classes, like 6-7, 6-8, and higher. Only one or two of my friends were in my class. As time passed, I lost touch with some of my elementary crew as we rarely saw each other and eventually built new friendships.

Sixth grade was a rough year in some ways. I learned again and again that we were the little guys. My crew got jumped at school, pushed around on the bus, and humiliated in front of the girls more times than I could count. The bus stop at Guzzlers became a dreaded place for us sixth-graders. I remember walking home with a Korean girl as she helped take out of my hair the gum that some eighth graders had spit on me as I got off the bus. It was so embarrassing, since I liked her and tried to get cool with her. But these days taught me how to grow up, be tough, and stand up for myself when I could — and learn to be quiet and take it when I was outnumbered.

Break dancing was still cool, and a few of us still did it at lunch. But it had reached its saturation point in American culture and quickly faded out. I was really disappointed because I loved it. As I looked around, I saw fewer people rocking the fat laces in their sneakers. But I still did. It seemed as if the whole hip-hop thing might fade out. Of course, it didn't; it just began to change. In fifth grade, I had started writing graffiti. As breaking faded

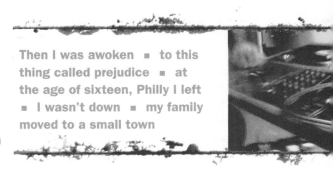

Then I was awoken ■ to this thing called prejudice ■ at the age of sixteen, Philly I left ■ I wasn't down ■ my family moved to a small town

out in middle school, graffiti became more of a focus as an outlet for my love of drawing. All of my book covers and my locker were tagged up with colorful bubble-letter graffiti art and characters. Art was one of my favorite classes.

Public school systems in urban areas are always less advanced than in the more affluent suburbs. Even though I rarely did any homework, I soon advanced to the top of my class. In seventh grade, I actually was the number-one student in my class, being on the distinguished honor roll with all A's and one B. The school wanted to move me up to 7-1, but I refused because all of my friends were in my class. In eighth grade, they moved me up to 8-2 because I continued at the top of my class. It motivated me to be the best. Several teachers really liked me and thought I had a bright future. I wasn't so sure about all that, but I did like some of the special attention. But in my high-school years, the good grades would change.

MUSIC IN MY BLOOD

Music was always a big part of my family. My mom was musically talented; she sang and played the piano and the organ. And my pops ... well, he tried to sing, but his brother Dave was part of a pretty popular singing group called the Couriers. Towering at 6'6", my uncle sang a deep bass. They had some pretty big hits back in the sixties and seventies and sold a lot of records. Yes, I mean vinyl records. In the eighties, my uncle's whole family started going out on the road together. They eventually developed a group called Homefire and traveled together after my cousins got married and had kids. At one time, they even had four large motor homes and traveled to churches to do concerts, workshops, and drama presentations on family. Today my uncle is approaching seventy, and he's actually back on the road again with his original Courier crew, connecting with their old fans. I guess once you have music and ministry in your blood, you just can't stop.

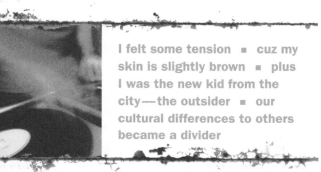

I felt some tension ▪ cuz my skin is slightly brown ▪ plus I was the new kid from the city—the outsider ▪ our cultural differences to others became a divider

My mother wanted me to learn how to play an instrument, so I began trumpet lessons in third grade. Mr. Alvarez was my instructor. This cat was a smooth jazz player who could play any instrument. He was bad! When I went to middle school, he transferred that year to the same school. I was so happy. He hooked me up with the middle-school band. By eighth grade, I found myself in the All Middle School Band, which was made up of the best players from all the middle schools in our section of the city. I was first-chair trumpet, which meant I was the best in our area.

During this time, I taught myself to play drums and started playing in the church services. The trumpet was cool, but I was really feeling the drums. I loved to freestyle and drop a beat to just about anything. Mr. Alvarez was really excited about my playing in the high-school marching band, but my parents had other plans. They wanted to send me to a Christian high school. At this time, I was a short skinny kid and had heard some terrifying stories about freshmen day at the public high school. Freshmen day was the dreaded day they violently initiated the new underclassmen. In eighth grade, I was cool and in control, but my memories of getting jumped and picked on when I was in sixth grade were still fresh. I knew being in ninth grade in the big high school would be really crazy. I was down to try Christian school, but when Mr. Alvarez found out, he was upset. He had a meeting with my parents to try to talk them out of it, but they were set. He actually walked out of the meeting cursing! In hindsight, that probably only further confirmed my parents' decision to go the "safer" Christian school route.

RHYMING ON THE BUS AND HEADING OFF TO JERSEY

More and more, we all heard rap on the radio and heard it played at school. My man Jeff was always spitting some lyrics at lunch from some of our favorite artists, like Run-D.M.C., the Beastie Boys, and local Philly heroes DJ Jazzy Jeff and the Fresh Prince (today known as Will Smith). Jeff started hooking me up with some mix tapes of their music, and I memorized all the words and rapped everywhere I went. Soon my pastime on the bus was spitting all the raps I knew to the girls and the fellows. People were feeling it and were amazed that I could memorize so many songs. I wrote some of my own lyrics a little bit here and there.

During the summer after eighth grade, I got ready to go to my new Christian high school, which was located over the bridge in New Jersey. I was a little nervous, which was made worse by the new braces I had on my teeth, but Christian school seemed like a much better option than the local high school, with freshmen day still in full effect. September rolled around and soon it was my first day at Life Center Christian Academy in Burlington. It definitely wasn't what I had expected, nor was it what the school expected either. That year LCA started accepting kids who got kicked out of public schools. A lot of these kids had serious issues. A Puerto Rican kid named George became my best friend at the school. This was his first year at LCA too, but his family went to church there, so he already knew a lot of the more popular kids. George watched my back, since I was the new kid. Even though this was New Jersey, this school was much more urban. I actually was one of the lightest-skinned kids in my class.

It was easy to see that the school had lost control of discipline. In my first nine years of public school, I had seen quite a few fights. But in my first three months at this Christian school, I saw many more. There were several fights every single day. The school would just issue detentions and meetings with the principal. At public school, when you got into a fight, you were immediately suspended. LCA realized they needed to make some changes. They soon implemented suspensions, and things calmed down some by Christmas.

Bus rides had always been a part of going to school, but they were usually not much longer than fifteen minutes. Going all the way to New Jersey took a good thirty-five to forty minutes on the bus. During my first year, there was only one other pickup in my area: an African American family with four kids. Shamee and Harry, the older ones, were my age. Shamee always brought the latest rap tapes with her and kept us all up on who was new. She was a big music fan. We always had our Walkmans for the long ride. Harry was into basketball, so we started playing ball together

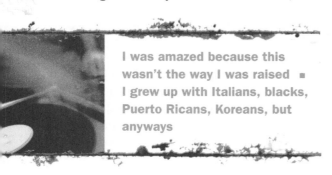

I was amazed because this wasn't the way I was raised ■ I grew up with Italians, blacks, Puerto Ricans, Koreans, but anyways

at my house in my broken-down driveway. When my tenth-grade year rolled around, they didn't come back to the school because their family couldn't afford it. The bus ride just wasn't the same. It was so quiet. But a few other new kids started coming, like Kim. She was one of my best friends from church, but everyone else at school just thought she was beautiful. All the guys tried to talk to her, and instantly my popularity rose because she and I were real close.

RAP MUSIC JUNKIE

As rap music and hip-hop culture grew, they really got ahold of me. By ninth grade, I was keeping up with them religiously. Every night, I listened to Power 99 FM in Philly play the Top 9 at 9. With a fresh cassette in hand (the days of CDs and iPods hadn't arrived yet), I'd try to catch my favorite songs and tape them so I could jam to them the next day on the bus and at school. Each of us bought the latest hip-hop albums and passed them around to our crew. When you made copies of a tape, it never sounded very good because there was a loud hiss in the background. We definitely weren't in the digital era back then.

As my love for rap music grew, it caused some controversy at home. I'd be banging it in my bedroom, and my parents would come in wondering what was with this crazy new music. They didn't like it one bit. In the late eighties, most mainstream hip-hop was fairly clean compared with main-stream hip-hop today. But it still had a few curse words here and there, and some of it was pretty blunt. As my parents listened to it, they caught a bad word or two. It was over. No more rap music for me. Not in their house. That didn't stop me, though. I just kept the volume low and snuck around.

HIP-HOP IN THE CHURCH

During this time, I wrote more of my own lyrics. My parents encouraged me to write lyrics for God. But I was caught up in my environment and wasn't really living a true Christian life. My heart had become somewhat hardened toward church and God. Nevertheless, writing lyrics for church was a chance for me to rap, so I started writing with some of my boys from church. During Christmas 1988, we had a chance to perform in front of a crowd. I had rapped on the bus, in the schoolyard, and in the hall, but I'd never really rapped with a microphone in front of a big audience. Wow, this was my big break! Well, not really. The crowd was mostly a bunch of gray-haired people who didn't have a clue about this new music genre. One Sunday night at the end of the service, my father said, "Well, we're now going to dismiss, but if you want to stay around, my son and some of the youth have written a Christian rap song. So if you want to check it out, you can stick around." Nobody moved. Everyone sat in their seats, curious. It was an awkward moment. We stepped on stage. My man Anthony Bruno,

aka Cool AD, was on drums, and Scott Kiple, aka KDM, rapped with me—Def Rap Tee. My mom played a little piano intro and a melody on the choruses. It was hilarious. I wish we had video of it, because it was classic. I'm sure there were some people who didn't know what to think of it. But at the end, we got a standing ovation accompanied by

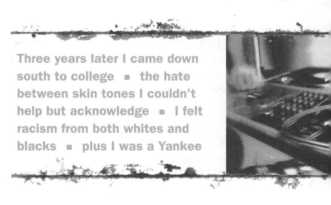

Three years later I came down south to college ■ the hate between skin tones I couldn't help but acknowledge ■ I felt racism from both whites and blacks ■ plus I was a Yankee

several amens. The Devastating Three was born. We would switch a few members around, but our big career was short-lived. We rapped two or three more times before a major change in my life took place.

MOVING TO THE MOUNTAINS

Our family had lived in Philly more than ten years, and my father felt like his time there was complete. God opened up the opportunity for our family to move to Chambersburg, Pennsylvania, about two and a half hours from the city. I was pretty torn up. Tenth grade had been great. I had played sports, built some close friendships, and even had a few girlfriends. Philly was my home. But I did have mixed emotions. A small part of me was curious about what a change would be like, although the bigger part of me really wasn't down with it. And once my friends and our church found out, I definitely didn't want to leave. Nobody wanted us to leave.

Unfortunately, things were really in turmoil that summer with my friends. A couple of them had run away, and several got in a lot of trouble. The girl I dated begged me to stay with her brother and work for him. He was one of the biggest drug dealers in the Frankford section of Philly. My best friend, Anthony, was upset that I was leaving, since we had become like brothers. Friends from my school in New Jersey couldn't believe I was leaving. Now it was a reality, and I really had mixed feelings. I almost made some stupid choices, but I decided to do the right thing and go with my family.

Our last Sunday at Northeast Assembly of God was a real emotional one—a lot of tears and standing room only. People shared songs, stories, and much gratitude for our family. Those people definitely loved us. After service, there was a big dinner with all kinds of great ethnic food. A few days later came the final goodbyes, and we put our last boxes in the moving truck and were off to the mountains.

CULTURE SHOCK

We arrived at our new spot in August 1989, just a few weeks before I started eleventh grade. There was a Christian school two blocks from our house, and my parents decided that I'd go there since it also had a nice gym and a good sports program. I played ball a couple of nights in the gym. The basketball coach met me and was really impressed—a short guy from the city jumping up and hanging on the rim. None of the other guys at the school could jump like that. Everyone on the team was white, and you know the old saying, "White men can't jump"? Well, it's generally true, and it definitely was at my new school. But there was still some incredible talent and some really tall guys.

As the school year started, I noticed everyone looked different, dressed different, and talked different than where I was from. Everyone knew I was the new kid since my accent stuck out. For the most part, everyone was pretty friendly and curious, since I was so different. So here's this city kid sitting at the lunch table with his new classmates talking about one of their favorite pastimes—hunting. What did I know about hunting? I quickly realized that I lived in a whole new world.

Sports became my life because there wasn't much else to do. Just a few months before we moved, the new Franklin Mills Mall a few miles from my house in Philly had opened up. It had more than two hundred stores. Chambersburg had a mall with only about thirty stores. This small-town thing took some getting used to, though several of the seniors embraced me. They thought I was pretty cool and more mature than the rest of the juniors. I had seen and experienced a lot of things in the city that they never had. Where I came from, none of my friends had cars or even thought about getting a car when we turned sixteen. In fact, many of my friends' families didn't even own cars because they took the bus or the subway. Now I'm in this small town, and almost all of my classmates have cars. It was crazy! Suddenly I found myself actually rolling places with my friends and with some of the seniors. It was a new type of freedom I didn't have in Philly. So there were a few pluses, but surely a lot more negatives. Or so I thought at first.

For the first time in my life, I experienced some real prejudice. This community of about twenty-five thousand people had a little project area and a hood with some minorities who lived there. But things were not nearly as multicultural as I was accustomed to. People didn't mix together much. With my olive complexion, dark hair, and Latin features, I found I didn't always fit in with the white kids. Yet the black kids in the neigh-borhood didn't accept me at first either. Plus, I was heavily into hip-hop. Where I was from, everyone was into hip-hop. It was our culture and our identity. In this small town, it was con-sidered really only a black thing. So because of my music and the way I looked and dressed, I felt some

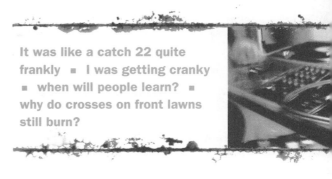

It was like a catch 22 quite frankly ▪ I was getting cranky ▪ when will people learn? ▪ why do crosses on front lawns still burn?

racism. In Philly, I hung out with people of all ethnic backgrounds, despite our differences. We would crack jokes and bug out with each other. But we focused on what we had in common, and our humor was never taken too seriously. Here, for the first time, I heard remarks, jokes, and even threats that were for real.

During eleventh grade, I soon found out how academically behind urban public-school systems were. In middle school, I was at the top of my class and on the Distinguished Honor Roll. When I went to Christian high school in New Jersey, it was definitely a lot harder, but I made the honor roll on and off. At my new school in a more rural part of Pennsylvania, I was barely getting by. In fact, I had to sit out from the basketball team for several weeks because my overall grade-point average was failing. I'd never had to deal with that before. I dove into my studies for hours and would really focus, but I still ended up getting a sixty-five or a seventy on a test. Some of the other guys in my class studied for a half an hour and got a ninety-five. It was a frustrating and humbling experience. I had to ask for some help because my classmates were so much more advanced. And during my senior year, I dropped some college-prep courses and took business classes instead. My grades improved little by little as I adjusted, but it was a learning experience in more ways than one.

MY FIRST REAL JOB

In Philly I had become a jack-of-all-trades, a hustler. I cut grass, raked yards, shoveled snow, and even cleaned doctors' offices with a cleaning company. As I got a little older, I began laying carpet with a guy from my church named Chris. He had accepted Christ at our church and our families became real tight. He became like a big brother to me.

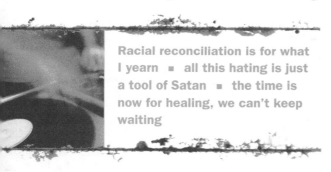

Racial reconciliation is for what I yearn ▪ all this hating is just a tool of Satan ▪ the time is now for healing, we can't keep waiting

When we moved to Chambersburg, it was time to get a real job. There wasn't really much to do in the small town, so I figured I could at least get a job and save up for the future. A lady in our church told us they were hiring Christmas workers at JCPenney at the little plaza mall only seven blocks away. A few days after I submitted my application, I interviewed with them and was hired on the spot. My official title was men's stock worker, and all I had to do was keep the men's department stocked and clean. As Christmas got closer, the store got busier and things quickly got out of place and bought up. I was constantly refilling everything and straightening up. Immediately the boss and managers noticed how good the men's department was looking. Many of the retail workers were middle-aged women and much different than me, but soon this city kid grabbed a special place in their hearts.

The store usually let the extra help go after the Christmas season was over, but they called me into the office and told me they would like to keep me and train me to work the registers. I was excited but at the same time a little nervous. Now I would have to deal with the customers all day and handle money. Fortunately I soon got the hang of it and loved it.

By my senior year, I moved over to the men's suits department and began to work on commission. My people skills really had to step it up. Here's this kid from Philly who loves sneakers and jeans now wearing suits and helping small-town men twice his age pick out suits and coordinate them with shirts and ties. I was definitely out of my element, but I really began to enjoy it because it was a challenge and it was great money for someone my age. People really get a kick out of it when I tell them that I used to wear suits to work every day. Most people see me dressed casually seven days a week—yes, even on Sunday—and can't imagine me all suited up. Yet JCPenney was a great experience that God used to get me out of my box and out of my urban world to help me see things from a different perspective, to see people from a different perspective.

MY RELATIONSHIP WITH GOD

Even though I had grown up in church my whole life, my relationship with God was very shaky. During my high-school years, it was virtually nonexistent. My heart became numb toward church and God. I had been around them so much. There were moments at camp or youth convention when I'd be inspired to make some changes and get committed, but when I got home, that fire quickly went out and it was back to the street mentality. I knew how to play the game and play it well. The people at my church thought I was just a great young man who played the drums with the worship team and even wore a suit and tie on the days he had to work after service. Inside, I knew it wasn't real, and my friends knew it wasn't real. But God never stopped tapping me on the shoulder even though I pushed him away for many years.

In December of my senior year, our family visited my grandparents in northern New Jersey. It was the time in my life when everyone asked me what I was going to do with my future. When I was younger, I had it all figured out: an artist, an architect, even a weatherman! But as I approached eighteen, I was clueless. The more people asked me about what college I was going to or what was next for me, the more nervous I became about my future.

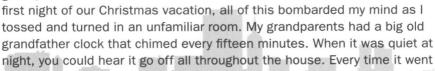

We're all equal, we're all the same ■ Christ's blood was for the black, the white, the Jew, the Gentile, the free, the slave ■ let's squash all the stereotypes in Jesus' name 77

As I lay in bed in my grandparents' house the first night of our Christmas vacation, all of this bombarded my mind as I tossed and turned in an unfamiliar room. My grandparents had a big old grandfather clock that chimed every fifteen minutes. When it was quiet at night, you could hear it go off all throughout the house. Every time it went off, I was determined to get to sleep before it went off again, but then it would chime again and again and again. It got to the point where I was counting. As it got later and later, I called out to God to let me figure out my future so I could get to sleep and have some peace. Going to a Christian college kept popping in my mind, but I had other ideas and kept pushing it out. It seemed as if I was wrestling with God in my mind. I couldn't even see myself at college, and certainly not a Christian one. Around 4:00 a.m. was a pivotal moment in my life. I finally submitted and told God I would do whatever he wanted if he would just let me stop worrying and get some sleep. I never heard the chime at 4:15. Funny how God guided my life and taught me lessons through mundane things like sneakers and sleep!

3

The Transformation

High school was over. I graduated. I made it! Now I was off to Valley Forge Christian College just outside of Philly. What was my major? Undeclared. I wasn't sure why I was going there, but I knew God had made it pretty clear this was where he wanted me. My family was proud, but my mother was really sad to see me grow up and leave the house. Personally, I was really excited that I'd be on my own yet be only about forty minutes from Philly and my old crew. Almost every weekend, I headed down to Philly to stay with some friends. Even though I attended Bible college, there was a side of me that wanted to get out in the city and try new things. Going to clubs, hanging out on South Street, and checking out some parties became a regular thing on my Philly weekends. Soon several friends came up to the college a couple of nights a week to play basketball in the gym with me. Many of the other students were from the suburbs or the country, and most of them were pretty intimidated by my friends and me. Nobody ever messed with me or disrespected me in our dorm.

YOU DOWN WITH VFCC?

I developed a reputation at the school as something of a bad boy. I rolled with the misfits and their subpar GPAs. I did better than most of my friends, but I barely scraped by with a 2.7 GPA, good enough not to risk losing my grants. I also did other creative things to build up my reputation. During high school, I got interested in cutting hair. My parents bought me a set of professional clippers. Back then, fades were popular, so everyone got the sides and back faded up and blended in. After I came to VFCC, I spread the word that I cut hair. At first many were skeptical, so I talked someone into giving him a free cut, and then the line formed. After the first guy, it wasn't free anymore. I set up a barbershop in the dorm lounge, doing fades and picking up some cash. I had a monopoly on the black and Hispanic students because nobody else knew how to cut their hair.

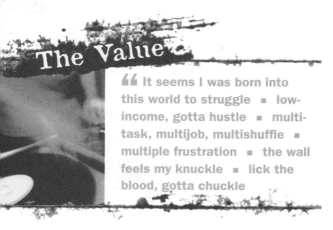

The Value

66 It seems I was born into this world to struggle ■ low-income, gotta hustle ■ multi-task, multijob, multishuffle ■ multiple frustration ■ the wall feels my knuckle ■ lick the blood, gotta chuckle

People also got wind of my other talents. The school started a talent show called JC Power House. A couple of guys wanted me to rap with them. I really hadn't rapped much since Philly, since Chambersburg never offered any real opportunities for me to grab the mic. But I knew I had it in me, so we switched up the lyrics from a popular song on the radio to make it a song about VFCC. When we busted out with "You Down with VFCC?" at the talent show, it was a big hit with everyone but the faculty. This was because at the end of the song, as I chanted the chorus, the other two guys got caught up in the moment and did a booty dance that some found offensive. Needless to say, we got banned from the next talent show. It was really pretty hilarious!

MY THREE WORLDS

Every third or fourth weekend, I'd go home to Chambersburg to see my family and my girlfriend. I would also talk to some girls in Philly on the weekends I went there. During this time in my life, I developed a player mentality. It became all about me in the midst of my new freedom and these three separate worlds that I was a part of—Chambersburg, school, and Philly. Even though I tried to follow God's plan by going to a Christian college, I was at the worst spiritual point in my life. I lied to my parents and several different girls, cheated on some of my tests, and developed an addiction to shoplifting. Experiencing freedom and new worlds quickly made me into another person. Inside, I knew all these things were wrong. Several times a week I had to sit through chapel services, but my heart was hard. I tasted these new freedoms in my new worlds, and I was becoming someone I didn't recognize.

We've all heard the saying that it's a small world. It's true! My different worlds collided, exposing secrets and crumbling foundations. A few girls from my church in Philly also went to my college. We never really hung out or talked much because they had a deeper connection with God. But apparently they knew about some of the things I was doing. Word got back to my old church and some people challenged me, along with my parents. These girls also had a friend who attended the same college my girlfriend went to, and she soon heard that I was talking to other girls. We already had a rocky relationship, so that was it for her. As the second semester started, she broke up with me, and it rocked my world. My parents also mistrusted me, but it didn't stop me. I covered it up by dating a few other girls and hanging out with my clubbing friends in Philly who weren't into God. Nevertheless, my uneasiness grew. God made me feel uncomfortable, and the things that used to cover up those feelings were no longer working.

As I sat in chapel on a Monday morning, I watched the crowd worship their creator. I felt like I was in a movie. What was I doing here? I was such a fake.

Could sing gospel like my famous uncle ■ but he wasn't raised on my street ■ didn't nod his head to this beat ■ I could be like my pops, but nah—he preach

Around me sat people preparing to go into full-time ministry as pastors, youth pastors, missionaries, and church workers. And here I was barely able to stand up, exhausted from my weekend of hanging out in the streets of Philly with friends who were headed nowhere. God spoke to me in that surreal moment. What was I going to choose? His plan? Or my own, a life full of so-called wonderful freedoms held together by smoke, strobe lights, and emptiness? His Spirit challenged me to step up or leave school. Either get with the program, or quit, get a dead-end job in the city, and hang out with my crew. I wrestled with these thoughts, tried to shrug them off, but they wouldn't go away. In my heart of hearts, I knew I needed to change, but I didn't know where to start. I had tried so many times, but over the years, my heart had become numb.

SERVING IN THE CITY

God took over and planted some people in my life to challenge me and get me involved in some simple ways of serving. A few girls asked me if I would be part of a new homeless ministry that some of the students started in the subways in Center City Philadelphia. They knew I was from Philly, and they really wanted someone involved who had some street smarts. I was down, and this made me feel needed.

I had never really given feeding homeless people much of a thought, but I was curious to see what it would be like. It was definitely a life-changing experience. We went down every Tuesday night at 10:00 p.m. in the winter and spring of 1992. A crack epidemic had infested inner cities across the country. Most of the guys in the subway were actually in their twenties—not much older than me—and they were all into hip-hop and street culture. They related to me more than the others because of the way I dressed and carried myself. They remembered my name each week.

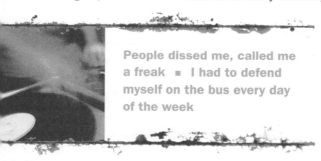

People dissed me, called me a freak ■ I had to defend myself on the bus every day of the week

Everything was cool until about the third week, when a couple of the guys asked me to pray with them. I panicked. The pastor's kid who grew up in church was scared to pray for someone. I called over some of the other students and asked them to pray for the guys.

One of the guys said, "No, Tommy, we want *you* to pray for us!"

"Me?" I replied.

"Yeah, come on, bro, say a prayer for us!"

I felt unworthy. Here I was trying to get my life together and these guys looked up to me as a spiritual leader. By this time, the crowd had grown to about fifteen people. So I bowed my head and asked God to help me before I prayed out loud. Giving out sandwiches and blankets was a cool ministry, because it was meeting a need and communicating God's love to people. But that night when I prayed, a realization hit me: my true purpose is leading others to Christ.

Around this time, my friend Rich, a senior about to graduate, had already started youth pastoring at a church in the city. A funny dude, Rich played practical jokes, would bug out, and was just fun to be around. Even though I wasn't always on-point, Rich never judged me. He still reached out to me and believed in me. I looked up to him because he knew where he was going. Rich was a true believer who knew how to have a good time while still representing Christ. He invited me to help him out with his youth ministry, because there were several urban kids he felt I could help reach. Again, I felt needed.

So here I was in the subways on Tuesdays and at a youth group on Wednesdays, building relationships with teens and young adults and trying to help them get their lives on-point while I was doing the same with mine. God worked in my heart as I built more of a real connection with him through my daily quiet time, seeking his will for my future. During that first year of college, I got sidetracked quite a bit. But God kept bringing me back

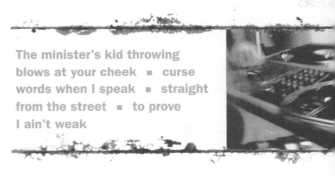

The minister's kid throwing blows at your cheek ■ curse words when I speak ■ straight from the street ■ to prove I ain't weak

to the point where I listened to what he had next for me. It soon became clear he wanted me to do urban ministry. I loved doing what I did at the youth group and in the subways. For the first time in my life, I felt true purpose and meaning. Something inside clicked. It all fit. It all made sense.

MIGRATION TO FLORIDA

Now there were some big decisions that I needed to make. I felt I needed a change in environment, so a college transfer was in the plans. It came down to two schools, one in the Midwest and one in Florida—cold weather in a boring small town or sunshine and beaches. Florida was farther from home, but God pushed me in that direction. (The weather didn't hurt, either.) In the fall of 1992, my family drove me down to Southeastern College (now University) in Lakeland, Florida. They were excited for me because I now had real direction and a better relationship with God.

A major reason for the transfer was for me to get away from my old environment and my old friends. My new roommate was Steve Mason, another transfer student from my old college. We were good friends and even knew each other from before college, when we both attended some retreats for pastors' kids. He also tried to make some changes, so we made a pact to go down to Southeastern together.

AN UNORTHODOX LIFE: MY STORY

Despite the move to Florida, my spiritual world was far from stable. Most of the new friendships I built were with people in the same spiritual state as me or worse. And I turned to the same things I was trying to get away from back in the city. It was a different club, different crew, different place, but the same old stuff. A geographical change can be a great help, but even more important is a change of heart. Though I had made some changes, some old ways still held on. I didn't have a different heart yet.

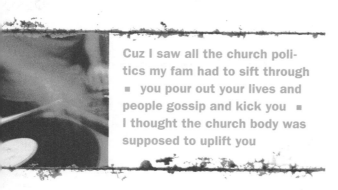

Cuz I saw all the church politics my fam had to sift through ▪ you pour out your lives and people gossip and kick you ▪ I thought the church body was supposed to uplift you

Around this time, I met a girl I had seen and even said hi to a couple of times. I knew she lived off campus, but she was mysterious and mostly kept to herself. I talked to and even hung out with a few girls here and there, but no real interest had developed. I still had a girlfriend back in Chambersburg, but we knew that our long-distance relationship probably wouldn't work. We committed to tell each other if anyone else came along. And I was open to whatever God wanted. One day that "whatever" happened. I finally met the mystery girl: Lucy Laguerra from Queens, New York. We kicked it for a good ten minutes before our next class. She was beautiful and interesting, and she found me interesting as well. We said we'd see each other around and parted ways. Inside, I jumped for joy, but I also kicked myself for not getting her phone number. I was worried that I wouldn't see her again for another week because her appearances were quite spotty. But the next day in chapel, we bumped into each other, and she asked me where I was sitting. From there, it was on! We soon developed a great friendship. We sat together in chapel, walked each other to some classes, and hung out on campus.

Lucy was two years older than me and seemed more focused about her future. She was smart, which was rather intimidating to me. A few weeks later, I finally got the nerve to ask her to go to the infamous Lake Hollingsworth to walk around the lake, a perfect place for poor college students to go on a free date. As we walked, we talked more about our lives, our goals, and our futures. There was really something different about Lucy. I had never felt this way about another person before. Even though I had dated several other girls and was pretty outgoing, I was scared to ask Lucy how she felt about me. I had my doubts that she wanted more than a friendship. Then a friend of ours pulled me aside and gave me the scoop that she really did like me. I needed that confidence booster. Soon after, we both shared how we felt about each other, and we officially started dating.

My relationship with Lucy came at a pivotal point in my life. God really pushed me to step up and give up all of the old things that still lurked around in my life. Lucy encouraged me, even though she didn't realize it at the time. She helped me get more focused on my walk with Christ, my classes, my ministry, and my future.

ROCKING THE MIC

Part of my new focus included participating in student ministry, which was required by the college. I got involved in the juvenile detention center ministry. Earlier in the semester, I had organized a rap group to perform at the school talent show. A few months later, our rap group had the opportunity to minister at the JDC. The presentation of our music and our testimonies connected with the kids. It was the best night of ministry we had seen at the JDC. The message we shared was the same one these kids heard every week during their chapel service, but in a different style. It clicked with them, and God

> You ever get picked for sports and cats skip you? ■ you ever had a teacher falsely rip you? ■ the street-corner thugs trip you? ■ get jumped and get a bloody lip too?

did his thing. The next week, I went to the student-ministry director to see about developing a new ministry for our rap group. He was over seventy years old and had no idea what rap was. I tried to explain it, but he was somewhat skeptical. As the semester went on, we ministered at a few other places, and apparently the word got back to him. By the next semester, we had become an official ministry that went to outreaches, churches, and prisons. The ministry director called us his "rap team." We laughed about it and gave our ministry more of a hip-hop name, Urban Disciples. It was incredible to see God breaking down walls. We had the opportunity to minister several times each semester in a variety of events, a huge blessing preparing me for my future ministry.

LOOKING NORTH

By my senior year, Lucy and I were pretty serious and started discussing our future. We knew we would eventually get married, and we hoped to move back up north to do ministry. Florida was a cool place to visit, vacation, or go to school, but not to live. Or so we thought. Each ministry major was required to do an internship, so I figured mine would be in New York City or Philly. As I shared this with the coordinator, he said they had nothing open in the Northeast because most of the school's connections were in the Southeast. I was disappointed, but I kept praying, because I really thought God would open something up. This was his plan, right? The coordinator encouraged me to try a few internship interviews with pastors to get some experience. An interview was set up for me with a pastor from Clearwater, Florida. I decided to go for the interview, but Clearwater? That's not urban. It's where we went to the beach. I assumed it would just be a waste of time.

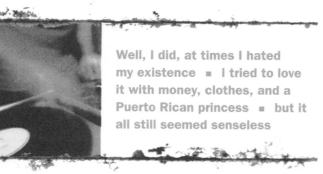

Well, I did, at times I hated my existence ■ I tried to love it with money, clothes, and a Puerto Rican princess ■ but it all still seemed senseless

As the interview began, the pastor shared his plan. He needed an intern to work in the community with the youth and the families. He explained that the church was built about twenty years ago, and the neighborhood had changed. It had become lower income and more urban, consisting mostly of minorities. He described the government housing down the street and how his entire congregation drove in from other parts of Clearwater and Pinellas County. The entire time he was sharing this, God sort of slapped me in the face a bit and stirred me up inside. I was surprised, to say the least. Then the pastor asked about my passion, my experience, and my abilities. I couldn't believe it! It seemed like a perfect fit. Even though I was convinced I would be doing an internship up north, God flipped the script and put me in Clearwater, Florida, of all places.

ENGAGEMENT, INTERNSHIP, AND FAMILY ISSUES

My life was quickly changing. My college years were coming to a close, and my future was at hand. It was both an exciting and a scary time. Lucy and I had been together for nearly two and a half years, and we knew God had brought us together for life. On Good Friday in April 1995, I took Lucy to Honeymoon Island and broke out an Easter basket with a bouquet of roses. Inside the bouquet was a poem asking her to marry me. Also inside the bouquet was a velvet rose whose top popped off to display the ring! She said yes, and it was official. We were engaged!

During this time, my parents had left their church in Chambersburg without another ministry lined up. A few months later, my father began working his first secular job in over thirty years. It was a really tough time. They seriously struggled while I was a thousand miles away doing my internship, preparing to get married, and in limbo about where I was going to do ministry when I graduated in six months. All the stability I had always experienced in my family life was now really shaky. We all had to fully rely on God and trust him for what was next. Inside, it hurt to watch my parents move in with my grandparents and wrestle with what God was doing in their lives. They were out of money, and my father made next to nothing working at a temporary factory job, mostly with immigrants who didn't speak much English.

Yet despite my family's difficulties, Clearwater First Assembly of God was a great experience for me. In the midst of all the other uncertainties in my life, it brought some normalcy as several people and families really embraced me. The church had a game room with about fifteen large video games, pool tables, and ping-pong tables. I started an open game room on Saturdays for the neighborhood teens. About twenty started coming each week. However, a few weeks after I got to the

I tried to be hard ■ put up my guard ■ but I was defenseless ■ God's relentless ■ I finally got to the root of the issue

church, the youth pastor, who had been there only one year, resigned. The pastor called me in and told me that the youth ministry and its sixty teens were now my responsibility. It was only for a month or so, since they were working hard to find someone quickly, but this was a huge undertaking for me, the intern. I was about to launch a neighborhood basketball league to reach a lot of teens from the community, and there was a lot on my plate, but I was eager and up for it. I was ready to serve.

The three-on-three basketball league started with more than sixty teenagers. A woman in the church sponsored the league with T-shirts for each team. We also promised each teen a free pair of sneakers if they completed the season—one of the main attractions. The league sponsored a pizza party tied in with the Wednesday night youth service. More than forty new teens from the community came, and the youth service was packed. Several made commitments to Christ. A good number of neighborhood teens started coming to the youth service and even on Sundays. The church was excited to see all the new kids, and the pastor was pleased to see some color in the church, since his previous church was multicultural. Yet it was difficult to cater to both crowds in the Wednesday night youth service. The majority of the church kids were pretty dead,

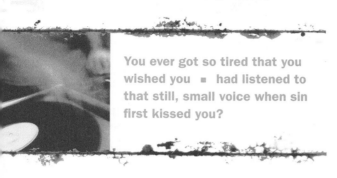

You ever got so tired that you wished you ∎ had listened to that still, small voice when sin first kissed you?

while the neighborhood teens were excited and participated in everything. The differences didn't come from race but from economic and cultural differences. These teens were from two different worlds. Some connected with each other. But most of them stayed in their separate groups. I was torn because I knew I was supposed to fill the gap while the church looked for a new youth pastor. But I related so much more with the neighborhood youth because of my background and because of their receptivity. Overall, the summer was a great experience and the youth group actually grew in numbers. Several people, including some of the staff, told me to apply for the job. Again, I was torn. This was a great church with a lot of great people who really embraced me as family. But I just didn't feel at peace in my spirit. I knew my calling was strictly for unchurched urban youth, not the suburban church kids. If they had created a position to reach the urban youth, I definitely would have considered it. But the timing wasn't right.

It seemed so exciting until she dissed you ∎ you were surprised you discovered your first love missed you ∎ well that was me and Jesus

At the end of the summer, we closed out the league with a big awards ceremony during a Sunday morning service. This was the day we presented more than sixty players with brand new Nikes. All summer I hustled to get donations from different businesses to help purchase the sneakers. It got a little discouraging and nerve-wracking at times because I faced a lot of rejection. But God hooked it up and did some real miracles. A couple of businesses in the church donated money, but I was still almost two thousand dollars short. A car dealership I had visited became an answer to our prayers—and we were really praying. They donated fifteen hundred dollars to help us pay for all the sneakers. The news stations showed up the day the dealership presented a big check at the church service. It was an incredible day. Close to two hundred visitors from the community showed up along with the teens and their families for the special presentation, during which each player was presented with a plaque and a pair of new sneakers. The crowd was a real diverse mix! It was an exciting day that I'll never forget.

What was next? I was unsure. My final semester of school started in a few weeks, and I didn't have the funds to pay for it. My family couldn't help me because they were barely getting by. So much of my life was completely up in the air. Then a guy by the name of Al Palmquist invited me out to lunch. He lived in Clearwater and had driven by the church on one of the basketball nights, and he was amazed. Years earlier, he had attended the church, but he was frustrated that they never reached out to the neighborhood. He was excited to see it happening now. At lunch, he shared with me about the church he attended in Tampa. They had a strong sidewalk Sunday school ministry with children in the housing projects, but they didn't have a youth program. He asked me about my plans. I told him I was uncertain.

My mom Elisaphos Givas prayed with believers that someday I'd truly receive this before I was selfish and shallow blinded to the value

At the end of service the next Sunday, the pastor shared about my needing financial help for my last semester of college. I was blown away. I had no clue he was going to do this. The people responded generously. Once again, God came through and did his thing, and most of my school bill was taken care of. A true miracle! Even though things had been stressful and up in the air, I began to see God work it all out. I just had to learn to trust. That's really difficult for a guy like me, who likes to have everything planned.

In October, I went to Tampa to do a sidewalk Sunday school program with Al Palmquist. That day, I met Pastor Joe McCutchen and checked out Crossover Community Church. We had a great time of ministry, and God started to tug on my heart. Could Crossover be the place? I didn't know. In the beginning of November, Pastor Bill Wilson from Metro Ministries came from New York to speak in our chapel service at school. This brother shared a message I'll never forget. He shared from the book of Amos about a shepherd who pulled his sheep out of the lion's mouth. Throughout his message, he intertwined heartwrenching stories of children and adults he worked with in Brooklyn. God was once again refreshing my calling. It was urban. It meant sacrifice. It meant real faith.

After letting that word marinate in my spirit, I called Crossover and said I was ready to start their youth ministry from scratch in the hood of Tampa. The church committed to pay me a big salary—a hundred dollars a month. Al jumped in and committed to support me with five hundred dollars a month, which for part-time seemed cool. I figured I could get another part-time job for a while. God saw my heart and my willingness. As I finished up my internship in Clearwater, the pastor told me they would be interested in supporting me as an urban missionary. They supported me with another six hundred dollars or more every month. It was just enough for me to be full time, since my future wife also would be working.

> But his lasik surgery opened my spiritual eyes so now you ■ can see, even with my father on his death bed ■ it can be best said ■ through it all I've learned to trust and be Christ led **"**

Suddenly, this shaky future came together in every area of my life. My family and I had been through a dry desert season, and now we were coming out of it. My father got a new ministry position as the senior pastor at a church just outside of Pittsburgh. When I went to visit during my Christmas break, I saw how great and welcoming his new church was. They were incredibly loving people! It had been a crazy year, but now everything was coming to a close. My college education was complete, my ministry was about to launch, my parents were at a new ministry, my school bill was paid, and I was about to get married. The next chapter of my life was about to begin.

4

A Place Called Crossover

Everything I owned was packed into my low-riding 1982 Chevy Cavalier hatchback. My stereo blasted some underground Cross Movement tracks as I pulled in the pastor's driveway in Tampa, Florida. It was January 1996, and I had just arrived in my new city. Pastor Joe and his wife, Judy, let me stay with them for the first month while I looked for an apartment and prepared to get married the following month. The next morning, Joe woke me up early and took me out to breakfast at his favorite breakfast spot. As we sat there eating our instant eggs, we discussed the church and its potential. After breakfast, we headed over to the church and Pastor Joe said something to me that I'll never forget. He didn't plan on staying at Crossover forever, just for a season. Joe had started several other churches and parachurch organizations and then moved on. He looked at me and said, "You're going to be the pastor at Crossover someday."

That was a pretty scary statement for me to hear on my first day of becoming the youth pastor. I said, "No, man. I'm called to youth ministry. Maybe when I'm like fifty, I'll be a pastor, but youth will be my thing for a long time."

Joe responded, "Don't worry. Not right now, but in about five years or so, you'll be the guy."

I laughed and said, "No way! I'll still be in my twenties!"

Despite my reservations, our conversation showed me how much Joe already trusted me. In a short period of time, we grew pretty close.

Crossover had been started just a few years before by a group of people who were fed up with organized religion. They were tired of the politics, the man-made preferences, and all the garbage that goes on in traditional churches. They were burned out. As they looked around Tampa, they saw a lot of people in the urban areas being ignored by the church as a whole. They wanted to make a difference. Pastor Joe had led some large traditional churches in the past, but God touched his and his wife's heart to reach out to the streets. Crossover was a different church. Pastor Joe was a real dude who wore jeans and T-shirts during the week. On Sundays, he'd dress up a little bit, but he still rocked an earring—quite progressive

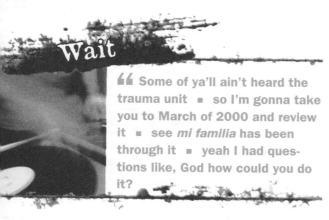

Wait

44 Some of ya'll ain't heard the trauma unit ▪ so I'm gonna take you to March of 2000 and review it ▪ see *mi familia* has been through it ▪ yeah I had questions like, God how could you do it?

for a pastor in the nineties. But it was easy to see that God was doing something new and fresh in this small church-plant. Authentic change took place in the lives of people who struggled with drug addiction, divorce, and wounds from the traditional church. This is where God had placed me, and I was ready to get it on.

There wasn't a lot for me to do the first month, so I set up my office and worked on some plans I'd be implementing. Two weeks later, I had my first youth meeting. Four young teenage girls came: two Asian girls who were Pastor Joe's neighbors, one African-American girl from sidewalk Sunday school, and one white girl whose dad actually attended the church. This was my new youth group. It was humbling, but fresh. I excitedly shared my story with them and some of the things that we would do for teens. I asked for their feedback. They thought I was cool, but they didn't believe that we would have many kids coming around. Of course, none of them had ever been in a church youth group before, so they were open for anything. That was perfect.

During the day, there wasn't much to do, so I did some day labor. That could be another chapter in itself. Long story short, I dug ditches—actual ditches—with alcoholics and drug addicts. Those were definitely some interesting days, but God humbled me and created opportunities for me to let my light shine.

TYING THE KNOT!

February 10, 1996, came fast, and Lucy and I got married at Iglesia de Dios. Over three hundred people gathered at her parents' Spanish church in East Tampa, where they now lived. Our friends and family came from Philly, New York, Puerto Rico, and from all over Florida. It was awesome to be with so many of the people we were close to. I was warned that Puerto Rican weddings never start on time, but I began to worry when Lucy was close to an hour late. Finally, we got the ceremony started, with Pastor Steve Lambert (the pastor from my internship) and Pastor Paul Kyllonen officiating. It was really special to have my dad there. It was a beautiful wedding with the music, the spoken words and prayers, the presence of our friends and family, but I just couldn't wait for it to be over and for all of the pressure to be off. After I kissed my bride, all of my groomsmen held up score cards rating our kiss. The crowd cracked up. We had a fun reception as my boys Johnny Jamz and S.W.N. deejayed the event in downtown Tampa. That night, we stayed in a honeymoon suite at Walt Disney World, and the next morning, we headed out for our honeymoon cruise. It was an incredible seven days together that neither of us will ever forget. We honored God by staying pure until we married, and he has blessed us in so many ways.

> But I knew it ▪ wasn't him to blame ▪ although things weren't the same ▪ I felt the rain ▪ a blood vessel burst in my pops' brain

Late February, we arrived back in Tampa and were ready to really kick off the youth ministry. We got settled into our new apartment, which was five minutes away from the church. My wife got a job transfer and began working as a youth counselor at Bay Area Youth Services in Tampa. A few days later, while we were opening a bank account, we got into a conversation with the lady helping us. She had four teenagers and was looking for a good church for them to attend. They showed up that evening at our youth meeting, among twenty teens who showed up for our first night back. As we built relationships with the kids, we were excited to see God already working in their lives. Our group soon outgrew the small prayer room we were using, and we moved to the main auditorium. In May, we moved youth group to Thursday nights so we could have the entire building, and we drafted a few people from the church to help us as the group grew.

THE NORTH TAMPA BASKETBALL LEAGUE

Around the same time, we started a basketball league with the City of Tampa. The parks department couldn't believe that I wanted to put on a free league and commit to get sneakers for all the teens who played the whole season. They were really blown away. The only thing we needed from them was permission to use their courts. They agreed, and more than eighty teens joined the league—a huge response. Each week, I lugged out a portable sound system to announce which teams would be playing on which courts. Truth be told, the main reason for using a sound system was to blast some Christian hip-hop and introduce these kids to Christ. A few weeks later, we had a basketball-league pizza party on a Thursday night at Crossover. Little did these kids know they were actually coming to our youth service. Our numbers more than doubled when more than seventy kids came out. We had some crowd-breakers and some games, plus I rapped and shared my testimony. Several teens responded to accept Christ. Most of these kids knew me as a coach or as the DJ who brought out the music during the basketball games. Now they saw the real me: the youth pastor. At the end of the league, we had a ceremony at Crossover that included more than sixty teens—more than half from the housing project and low-income homes—receiving brand-new Reeboks and nice wall plaques.

I never would have began to entertain ■ these horrific thoughts or tear drops ■ I got rocked ■ to discover his heart stopped ■ over four minutes

We ran a few other leagues after this initial one, but the main purpose was to build relationships in the community and initiate a presence. From that presence, our Thursday night teen service really grew. By the end of the first year, we averaged around sixty teens. We bused in many of these kids to the church in our old 1973 van, known around the hood as the Hooptie. Over the next two years, the youth group remained at about the same number of teens, with Lucy and me serving as the main leaders. A few other people helped out for a season, but many of them didn't stick around after the initial "wow" wore off. It was exciting that a lot of urban kids came to church, but once people saw how many issues these teens had, they were overwhelmed. Some rough kids attended, most of whom had never been in church before. The majority also came from fatherless homes in drug-infested neighborhoods. They needed extra attention and love.

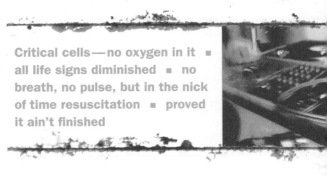

Critical cells — no oxygen in it ■ all life signs diminished ■ no breath, no pulse, but in the nick of time resuscitation ■ proved it ain't finished

The nearby Riverview Terrace housing projects and the area around them was a crazy place in the late nineties. Every week, I visited teens and played basketball at the park in the projects. During my visits, I regularly encountered drug deals, drug addicts, fights, and gunshots. These projects were less than a mile from the church. To many of the teens, I became like a big brother or even a father figure, since most of the males in their family had left, had been killed, or were in prison. As you looked around the streets, there were no men over the age of twenty-one.

By our second year of youth ministry, we had a core of urban teens committed to Christ. It was exciting to watch their lives being transformed despite their circumstances.

KEEP IT REAL, THE ANSWERS, AND THE MISSIN' ELEMENT

Shortly after I arrived in Tampa, my pastor encouraged me to record a hip-hop album. Around the same time, God put some brothers in my life who believed in me and wanted to pour into me. So each week, I traveled over to South St. Pete to a bedroom studio at Johnny Havel's house (aka Johnny Jamz). His partner Marty (S.W.N.) produced beats for my first solo album. Being a persistent dude, I would wake Marty up at 11:00 a.m. after he had worked at Subway until 3:00 a.m. We completed the album in about six months, and I pressed up my first three hundred tapes of *Keep It Real*. We were all really excited, since I also featured some friends on the album. I had always dreamed of recording an album and being able to share my story, and now it was a reality. Soon God opened up all kinds of doors for me to rap at different events across the Tampa Bay area. Within three months, the tapes sold out, and I pressed up five hundred more, along with five hundred CDs.

In 1997, I worked on my next CD, *The Answers*. This time, I had a lot more knowledge and stepped it up in several ways. Before the album released in 1998, I submitted a song to a national compilation called *Godzhouse.com*. My song "Roots" was accepted, and the album hit stores in the spring. It was really an honor just to be a part of the project, since several nationally known groups were on the album. My song featured Cruz Cordero, who was also from Philly. We rapped about our ethnicities and about being from Philly, but we focused on what we had in common—our relationship with Christ. The song soon ended up on some Christian hip-hop charts on the internet, which grabbed the attention of some up-and-coming record labels.

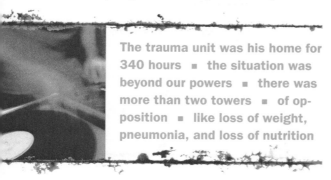

The trauma unit was his home for 340 hours ▪ the situation was beyond our powers ▪ there was more than two towers ▪ of opposition ▪ like loss of weight, pneumonia, and loss of nutrition

During the summer of 1998, I received a call from Seventh Street Records about possibly coming aboard with their new label. Shortly after, Seventh Street talked to the Cross Movement about signing them as well. John Wells, the leader of this movement, and I had several conversations with each other as we tried to feel out this new label to see what they were really about. We both took our time. They had to amend the contract to state that my touring schedule would not conflict with my commitment to the youth ministry at my church. The ministry was still my priority. If they weren't willing to agree, I was willing to turn it down. God honored that, as Dave Bunce and his wife from Seventh Street were cool with my priorities. The Cross Movement and I signed around the same time in the fall of 1998.

In December, I flew to LA to record my new album, *The Missin' Element*, and to shoot a music video. This major trip was full of first-time events for me—first time to California, first time in a real studio, first time shooting a music video. I asked God to keep me grounded and to keep my heart in the right place during this exciting and surreal time. Even though so many things around me were changing, I didn't want my motives and my character to change. After finishing most of the album in four days, we headed to the video shoot in Santa Ana. We arrived at 8:00 p.m. at this tattoo parlor. There was a tractor-trailer full of equipment, people building sets, hired extras, a food spread—the whole nine yards. I couldn't believe all of this was really going down. It was exciting, but I was disappointed that my crew wasn't able to be there with me to be in the video. Some of my friends, Sup the Chemist and Dirt from Cali, did join me for the shoot, though. The song was "Skintone," which deals with racism. The director created the concept around four people of different races separately getting tattoos. When each one looks in the mirror to see their new ink, there's nothing there. The scenes after that show all of them having fun coming together and interacting. The video symbolizes that the change Christ makes in our lives is really on the inside and that we're all part of his family no matter what our skin looks like. A deep but fitting message.

PASTORAL CHANGES

In the middle of all this great music stuff, the church went through a serious transition. Pastor Joe took me out for a ride and broke it to me that he was leaving. I didn't see it coming. Joe had shared that he wouldn't be at Crossover forever, but I didn't think it would come this fast. He assured me that everything would be okay and that this guy who had been a regular guest speaker would take his spot. The youth ministry would keep going forward. Honestly, it would have been a perfect time for me to leave too. I was in the middle of signing a national record deal, and things at the church were in transition. "God, are you trying to tell me something?" No. That's not what he was trying to tell me, although it did seem to make some sense.

The new pastor was much younger and was supportive of the youth ministry. This brother had a phenomenal knowledge of the Scriptures and had some great plans for the church. But he had another job, working up to sixty hours a week in a management position. He also had a family with two children. Although he had plans to phase out his other job and work more at the church, it wasn't an easy thing to make happen. The church was small and so were the finances. For nearly two years, he tried to make the transition, but it was difficult for him because of his demanding schedule. By the summer of 2000, he was burned out and had moved on.

My faith was in transition ■ from just mediocre to solid steel ■ see it looked hopeless and my parents had no insurance deal ■ with $430,000 in hospital bills, it gets real

I vividly remember that next Sunday in July of 2000, just after he had left. Guess who had to preach that day? It felt weird to stand in front of the small congregation. But we were all in this together, and we weren't going to let things fall apart. We had a fresh breath of purpose. Even though there were only about forty people gathering on Sundays, the youth ministry had grown to a hundred and fifty on Thursday nights, and lives were being miraculously changed. Many of us had poured too much time, energy, and effort into this place to watch it go under. But I wasn't ready to be the pastor. I was sure of that. Who could pastor this uniquely urban church, which was becoming defined more and more by its thriving hip-hop-style youth ministry?

The same guy who initially brought me to the church from Clearwater stepped up to the plate. Al Palmquist had been an author and an evangelist for several years in the eighties. He didn't have much experience pastoring, but he believed in Crossover and was willing to help out even though he had a couple of other jobs himself. Even though Al was about thirty years older than the pastor who had just left, he connected with people much better. As a former vice cop in Minneapolis, Al understood the streets. He shared some incredible stories and miracles from a ministry he was part of in the Midwest. A great storyteller, Al engaged our increasingly urban crowd on Sundays. It also helped that he came to the Thursday night service and built relationships with many of the teens and the young adults. For the first time since I had been at the church, there was a real connection between Thursday nights and Sundays.

I'm trying to feel ■ some relief from all the grief and the tension ■ my emotions now exist on a different dimension ■ my moms can't sleep she's falling into a deep state of depression

THE TRAUMA UNIT

All this time, my parents supported me while they continued in ministry in Pennsylvania. They were a solid foundation for my life even when things got a little rocky. In March 2000, I got home late from youth service, and my wife was crying. She told me to sit down. My mom had just called her to say that my dad was rushed to the hospital. They didn't know what was wrong, but he was barely hanging on.

My father had never been sick before and had never even been to the hospital. He was healthy. How could this be happening? I broke. Over an hour later, my mom called back and gave us some details. He had a massive aneurism in his brain. A small blood vessel burst, shutting everything down. He stopped breathing, and his heart stopped beating for over four minutes. When the paramedics arrived, they resuscitated him, but he also suffered a stroke since his brain received no oxygen for several minutes.

He was flown by helicopter to the big hospital in downtown Pittsburgh. It didn't look good. My wife and I bought plane tickets and flew out the next morning.

Although I had lost some of my closest friends, this was definitely the hardest thing I'd ever been through. My parents' church supported us, but it was tough. I tried to be strong for my mom and my sister, since I was now the man of the family. My dad was in a coma and was hooked up to life support because of multiple complications. The doctors told us he could pass at any time. I was rocked. Although I had grown up in an urban world and saw others go through a lot of things, I always had a solid family life. This changed everything. It would never be the same again. My security blanket was stripped away. How could God let this happen? The questions poured out of my traumatized mind.

Not to mention ■ my sister's upcoming wedding ceremony ■ my father was gonna do it, but now I'm the only ■ man in the fam, and it feels lonely ■ asking the Creator to hold me

In the midst of all my questioning and crying out, God spoke to me. Not in some loud audible voice but in the stillness of my heart. I can't even put the experience into words, but he comforted me and let me know that everything was under control. It would be okay. I held onto that. But I had moments of doubt as more complications emerged.

We flew back to Florida after a week. After a month, my dad was moved from the trauma unit to intensive care. The doctors insisted he probably wouldn't come out of the coma, and if he did, they thought he'd be a vegetable because his brain scans looked abnormal. We prayed and trusted God through this time. That's really all we could do.

Shortly after, my dad got off life support and his trachea was closed. A few weeks later, he began to talk! Over the following months, he sat up, talked more, and even got to go in a wheelchair. It was amazing to see what God was doing.

My parents' church continued to pray and to support my mom in so many ways. Eventually the church decided to look for another pastor, since my dad's healing was taking some time. They were so gracious and loving toward my family. My mom moved with my dad to Georgia to be close to my sister, and my father was moved to a rehabilitation home close to where my mother lived. There were some difficult changes, and they stretched our faith, to say the least. I can't say that my dad is back to normal. But I can look at the positive side and see what God has done.

For me, the whole process has been the biggest example of God's people helping each other. My parents had no health insurance because they couldn't afford it. Over $430,000 in hospital bills had accumulated, and they had no way to pay. However, the hospital, a faith-based institution, had a grant program for ministers. My mom filled out the paperwork, and the hospital paid the entire

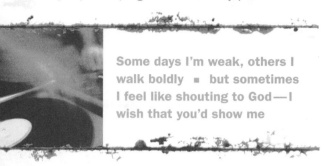

Some days I'm weak, others I walk boldly ■ but sometimes I feel like shouting to God—I wish that you'd show me

bill! There were still over fifty thousand dollars of other doctor's bills that the hospital couldn't cover, yet God met every single need. Churches and friends of my parents from all over sent encouraging letters, called, and sent money to help out. My mom went through a major depression and couldn't sleep for months. During that time, someone from the church stayed with her at her house. God has pulled her through and met every single need, helping her grow in so many ways. Recently my mom just bought her first townhouse in Georgia, and she's working and very involved in her church. She's become one of the strongest women I know. My dad continues to make progress at the rehabilitation home as we trust God and let him do his thing.

MORE CHANGES

About a year after Al had taken over, he took me out to lunch and said the church needed to start looking for another pastor or that I needed to step up and take over. I was shocked and terrified. Al and I were close, and I hoped he was venting a little bit because he was tired. I encouraged him and told him not to give up. I'd help in any way I could. Everything seemed to be okay for another month or so, but then he again expressed the need to me and then to some of the other leaders. Their response was the same as mine: "You can do it. Hang in there—we're a team." He was okay again for a little while, but his demanding schedule made him weary. The attendance on Sundays stayed about the same, and Al was feeling the reality that ministry can get discouraging. As the fall continued, the leaders felt uncertainty about the future of the church. Some members from the congregation sensed that something was up and slacked off in their attendance. In October, Al announced he was going to take a sabbatical for two months to figure out what he should do. Guess who was left in charge? Me. During this time, one of the other youth leaders, Jim

Dell, stepped up to help me out. Jim had worked with Metro Ministries in New York and had quite a bit of experience. He encouraged us, pushed us, challenged us, and brought some fresh perspective to the ministry during a pivotal season.

Although there were still only about forty people coming on Sundays, the faces of these forty people looked a lot different from when I first came six years before. Over thirty of them were young, multicultural products of the youth ministry. Many of them looked to me as their pastor, and during this time, many of them openly expressed that to me. It was scary because I knew Al leaned toward moving on. I felt pretty overwhelmed. I was a husband, a youth pastor to nearly two hundred people, a national hip-hop artist— what more could I really handle? I never wanted to be a pastor. My wife and I prayed about it and talked

But I've learned his timing is not the same as ours ▪ I'm talking about the CEO of the planets and stars

about it a lot. We came to the conclusion that it wasn't about us. The church needed a pastor, and God called us to step up.

One night in late December, I sat in my kitchen clutching the phone. Al had been like a father figure to me in many ways, especially since what had happened to my biological father. Here I was telling him I was ready to take his place. I was nervous. He told me he knew his time was finished and that it was time for me to take over. We had a pastoral council meeting coming up the following week, and he told me he would be stepping down and fully backing me.

BECOMING THE LEAD PASTOR

The new year, 2002, arrived. A few days later, we had our meeting, and it became official. I did the thing I had many times sworn I would never do. I became the pastor. It's funny how God works things out. He has a real sense of humor. My father was a pastor, and growing up, I'd always said I'd never do what he did. Now here I was: twenty-eight years old and doing it. It looked a whole lot different, but I was doing it. I grew up around church and had been in ministry full time for six years, so I had some idea of how to do it. But I didn't want to mess it up. I wanted to make sure we were following what God had for us. Crossover always had so much potential, but it never seemed to bloom for the church as a whole. Yes, the youth ministry took off, but here we were six years later, and the Sunday attendance was still the same. The church struggled to find an identity. There had been three different pastors within six years, and the vision varied quite a bit. And honestly, the vision was never all that focused, because the church was so small. Each pastor had to work another job or jobs to provide for their families.

Even with my experience, I knew this task was much bigger than my expertise. On the advice of others, I looked for some mentors. I met with a pastor who had started a church about ten years earlier and made a huge impact in his community by reaching people who didn't go to church. His church had grown to close to fifteen hundred. Although his church attracted a much different crowd, I knew the principles he followed were transferable. We started meeting every month or so, and I asked many questions. A lot of these dynamics were new to me. It was sometimes tough to grasp: I was now the guy in charge. I was now the shepherd, the one accountable before God for these people. It was scary, and in my mind, there was no room for error.

My mentor reintroduced me to Rick Warren's book *The Purpose Driven Church*. I had skimmed this book as a youth pastor. But reading it as a pastor, I engaged with it in a serious way. My spirit shouted in response to what I was reading, "Yes, we do that!" or, "That's why we do that," or, "We

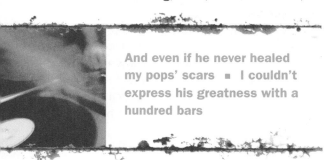

And even if he never healed my pops' scars ▪ I couldn't express his greatness with a hundred bars

really need to step that up." I was really vibing with it. Rick does an awesome job of clearly defining the New Testament church and how it should be a model for our churches today. The book points to the reasons why there are many un-healthy churches. They are not fulfilling the original purpose of the church. This got me excited. God used this book to give me some new purpose, some needed direction, and some fresh inspiration.

As I continued to seek God for our specific direction, it became clear that he wanted us to reach people affected by the hip-hop culture. That was what the youth ministry did, but could that really work as a direction for a whole church? Thirty of the forty people who attended on Sundays were younger adults who fell into that category, but still we were unsure. Even though the number one Arbitron-rated radio station in our city was a hip-hop station and the majority of the people in our community listened to this style of music, we still wondered. This had never been done before. There was no model. So the questions emerged: Is this really God's will?

Can we really do this? Can we use turntables on Sunday mornings? Can we ever become financially stable? We asked all kinds of questions, full of doubts. But we took some small steps and followed God's direction.

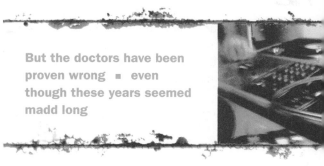

> But the doctors have been proven wrong ■ even though these years seemed madd long

Suddenly, people actually visited our Sunday service. We rarely ever had visitors. It was almost surreal as we stepped back and watched Sundays grow. Since there were visitors, we began to do invitations on Sundays for people to build new relationships with Christ. People responded every time. By fall 2002, our attendance had doubled to about eighty on Sundays, and the Thursday night service, which I continued to lead, was still rocking as well.

DEFINING THE MISSION

We had our first retreat for all the church leaders. By this time, God had clearly shown me the vision, and I felt confident enough to share it with the rest of the leaders. I shared in detail about our becoming a full-blown purpose-driven church that reaches hip-hop culture. The team was excited about the vision and excited about all the growth that began to happen. On Saturday, we dedicated the entire morning to coming up with a new mission statement for our ministry. We knew that we wanted to include the five purposes of the church in our statement, but we wanted it to define who we were trying to reach and how we were going to do it. At the same time, we wanted this statement to be understandable to anyone who walked into our church for the first time, so it was pretty challenging. About two hours later, through prayer, we hashed out the mission statement that is still in effect today: "To relevantly introduce the truth of Christ to the hip-hop culture as we develop worship, purpose, unity, and leadership in their lives." It was a defining moment for our ministry. We now had something that clearly told people what we were all about.

Now that we had a mission statement, we wanted to clearly communicate it to our people. We needed them to get behind it and get involved in serving God so that together we could accomplish the mission God had given us. At the end of 2002, we had our first membership class. Even people who had attended for years took part in it. We followed the blueprint of the membership classes at Saddleback Church in California. Of course, our team tweaked it so it would fit our audience and our cultural context. The purpose-driven model is a series of classes that moves people toward spiritual maturity and encourages them to make stronger commitments to Christ. It's been a phenomenal structure for us. We called our series Connection Classes, and more than sixty people came to our first one, even though it was during the busy Christmas season. It was exciting. It felt like the church was starting from scratch and this was a whole new day.

GROWTH CONTINUES

During the next year, we got more focused and organized as more and more people joined us. We started small groups and several new ministries for people to get involved with. Our family also grew, as my wife and I had our first child. We had a little girl named Deyana Luz (Divine Light). A healthy and happy baby, Baby D has brought so much joy to our family, especially since she was the first grandchild on both sides. My wife and I made the tough decision that she would not go back to work after the

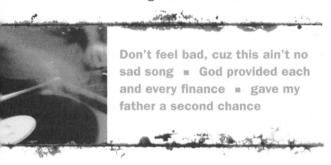

Don't feel bad, cuz this ain't no sad song ▪ God provided each and every finance ▪ gave my father a second chance

birth. As one of the directors at the Center for Girls, she worked with teens in the community. She was being led to raise our new daughter and to work at the church part time to help with administration. This was a real step of faith, since she had her master's degree and essentially was the breadwinner of the family. She would earn about a third of what she used to. But we trusted God. We didn't have any major debts because of our discipline, and we had planned for our first child for many years. Lucy became a real blessing to Crossover by putting new structure and new systems in place to handle the church's growth.

As 2004 rolled around, we had grown to the point that we ran out of space in our Sunday service. We prayed about adding a second service, but we didn't want to do it until it was absolutely needed. Most of our crowd doesn't like to get up early, so we wondered if adding an earlier service would even be feasible. And our team had a lot of questions about the dynamics of having two services. It seemed like it would be a lot more work. I talked with several other pastors who did multiple services to get some advice about making the transition. In March, we stepped out and launched our 9:30 a.m. service and pushed our 11:00 a.m. service to 11:15 a.m. We were surprised at how smoothly everything went. People were really happy about having an option. The change also freed up more space in the second service, because many people decided to come earlier. People who served in one service now had the opportunity to come and receive in the other one. And several new people started coming to the earlier service since they had to work at noon and hadn't been able to come to the eleven o'clock service.

GETTING MORE RELEVANT

So many things were already different about our church. Our singing and worship time had an R&B and hip-hop feel with a DJ spinning instrumentals from Christian groups on the turntables. We sang many songs that were common at other churches, but we did them with a remixed flavor. Our worship team, Harmony, also wrote several original songs and released several CDs with instrumentals for other churches to use as a resource in their services. We stopped using bright florescent lighting in the auditorium and installed recessed lighting with dimmers so we could make the room feel warmer and more like a big living room. During the worship part of the service, we dimmed the lights real low because our crowd felt more comfortable singing when it was not as bright. We covered the back wall of the stage and the windows with colorful urban graffiti art. We created a comfortable atmosphere where people could come casually dressed and be themselves. If you walked in on any Sunday, you'd see people wearing hats, do-rags, and braids with jeans and T-shirts sitting next to people wearing button-down shirts and khaki pants. Our crowd was and still is a multicultural mix of people from all different backgrounds. Although we were in Tampa, more than 80 percent were from up north and nearly half of our congregation came from New York City. Since Tampa is a growing emerging city, most people are originally

> All it did was enhance ■ our walk ■ inspire our talk ■ to encourage people from Germany, to Japan, to New York

from somewhere else. Crossover is a big melting pot, which really represents our community at large.

Although we presented a unique worship experience, we always strived to be relevant. We had creative planning meetings with some of our staff to plan our weekend services and add even more flavor. Of course, we touched on real issues that people deal with and showed them what God has to say about them and how to apply what he has to say to their lives.

In 2004, we started developing several message series aimed at the heartbeat of the culture, incorporating original short films that our media team produced. The whole dynamic of our services changed as we added video, songs, music, and conversation, along with the message.

We also added basketball courts and a large patio in the front section of the church. Mark Jannetta, our children's pastor at the time, also developed a skateboarding ministry. God did some real miracles and provided some funding from private donors to help build our ten-thousand-square-foot Splinter Skate Park (www.splinterskatepark.com). Mark has since moved on to lead Splinter's newly developed nonprofit organization with a team of interns and volunteers, producing resources for the skate culture and building other Splinter Skate Parks around the country. When he moved to the Midwest to continue to duplicate the model, he raised up leaders from our ministry to staff our park.

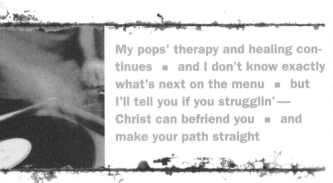

My pops' therapy and healing continues ■ and I don't know exactly what's next on the menu ■ but I'll tell you if you strugglin'— Christ can befriend you ■ and make your path straight

By this time, not only did our church look different, as we had remodeled the whole facility and added several features, but we also ran things differently in order to purposefully engage our community. As we were led by God's Spirit, lives changed and people reached out to others. Growth was contagious.

Of course, many challenges come with working with a mostly unchurched crowd, dynamics which we'll address later in this book.

GETTING CREATIVE WITH OUR SPACE

In spring 2005, we grew from three hundred to four hundred in our Sunday services. We were stretched for space again as our second service was at capacity. For a while we prayed about starting a Saturday night service, but we wanted to hold off as long as we could. The sacrifice would fall on me, since many of my concerts were on Saturdays. I'd have to cut almost all of those events out of my schedule. But the church was my first priority, so I was ready to do whatever it would take. We had to do something because we were out of space to grow. There were a few weeks when we placed chairs on the stage for extra seating. The other reason for a Saturday service was that a large portion of the people we were trying to reach didn't like to get up on Sunday mornings after being out late the night before. Yet another group worked on Sundays, and they weren't going to change their schedule to come to church, especially if they didn't have a relationship with God yet. Our hearts were burdened to reach these people and create more realistic options for them.

In July 2005, we launched a Saturday night service. Around the same time, we turned our Thursday night service back to a teens-only service. So many young adults were coming that we constantly ran out of seats each week. We encouraged the young adults to come out on Saturday night, since many of them didn't come on Sunday. Immediately, we gained several new people who hadn't come to our church before. But we soon found that Saturday night was real up and down: some weeks we had a decent crowd, and the next week it was half empty. Most of the young adults who came on Thursday night couldn't come on Saturday due to work or having so many other things going on. We tried several things to promote it and get the word out. It grew some, but it never developed like we had envisioned.

Although the attendance wasn't that bad, we noticed that half of the crowd or more was different each week. And we were really stretched for volunteers to run the service, since it was difficult to recruit from such a transient crowd.

> I know the language of pain ▪ so I can translate ▪ I know the love that he gives is beyond great ▪ so heavenly Father ... I put my dad in your hands — give me strength as I wait **"**

We prayed and talked with each other and with other ministries, and came to the conclusion that Saturday night wasn't the best option for our target audience. It may be in some places, but in Tampa there is a lot of stuff happening on Saturday nights. Yet we knew we needed to do something for that crowd. In the summer of 2006, we shut down the Saturday night service and built a team to relaunch our weekend evening service in the future on Sunday night. As we surveyed our crowd, most of them expressed that Sunday night would be easier to invite unchurched friends, since it's an "off night." The mall is closed, most businesses are closed, and there's nothing major to compete with. We did some unique things with our Sunday night service, like adding a guest artist, food, open mic, break dancing, and sometimes tweaking the weekend message to make it a little more evangelistic.

We must be willing to change. If you see something not working, or it's just mediocre, you must ask questions. Don't get comfortable. Because of our auditorium's limited capacity, we built another large patio with an awning on the back side of the church. We added cafe tables and a big screen, and it became our video cafe. People sit and watch the service while drinking coffee or eating snacks. This area seats over a hundred people and also serves as an overflow seating area. But several people just like to sit out in the outdoor atmosphere for something different. I encourage you to get creative with your space. If we had kept the mindset of having one service in one room, we would have stopped growing a long time ago.

WHAT'S NEXT?

Many say it's a miracle that we've built a solid self-sustaining community of faith in an urban/hip-hop context. We give God the credit for everything we've accomplished. What's next? What are our plans? This is a question we often hear. Crossover has become internationally known as the first authentic church model that is reaching the hip-hop culture. Because there are very few resources to equip leaders to reach this culture, we plan to continue to fill that gap. Crossover has developed several resources, including CDs, DVDs, curriculum, message series, books, and more.

When it comes to our facility, we know that God has an even greater vision for our church. Crossover plans to relocate in the near future to a main-street facility that will provide plenty of square footage, parking, and visibility. Our new campus will let us expand all of our current services, programs, and ministries while giving us the ability to add several new ones. When, where, and how are the questions! With every major project we've undertaken, these have always been the questions. But God has always answered them and provided for every need. Our story is filled with miracles, and although relocating will be our biggest challenge yet, we know that it will be an even greater opportunity for God to shine and get his props.

PART TWO

church ● **hip-hop** ● culture

An Unorthodox Culture

Hip-Hop's History

5

The South Bronx

Countless people groups around the globe have experienced intense times of oppression. In the middle of those tough times, people banded together and found relief in something or someone. They searched for a voice. A voice that would bring them to freedom, a voice that could bring them some inner peace, and many times a voice that would bring them revenge. This paints the picture of Jewish culture in the time of Christ's life, a group of people under Roman rule. Although they worshiped in their temple and abided by their laws, the Jews also had to adhere to Roman laws and live with additional taxes and the constant reminder of their inferiority to their Roman counterparts. The branch of Roman government in this Far Eastern province was full of lawlessness and corruption. The Jews were weary. Several movements and revolts were started, but each one miserably failed under the iron fist of the Romans.

Then Jesus emerged at the age of thirty with his impressive wisdom, supernatural miracles, and massive following. Could he be the one? Could he free his people from the clutches of Rome? People looked for a voice, a way out, vindication. Many banked on it. When Jesus talked about building his kingdom, people were ready to sign up. But when he broke down what he meant by his kingdom, many people's hearts dropped. He talked about his heavenly kingdom, not an earthly one. He came to offer spiritual freedom, not political freedom. In the middle of Roman oppression, many found something much bigger than what they were looking for. They found hope, forgiveness, and a reconnection with their creator. Oppressed people across the planet still connect every day with the promise Christ offers.

THE BRONX ECONOMY

Fast-forward to the 1970s. The South Bronx was experiencing a serious time of oppression. It didn't happen overnight but through a series of events that made the Bronx look like a third-world country. At one time, the Bronx had been a big community full of working-class people mostly of Irish, Jewish, and Italian descent. But New York City's master plan was to

Hip-Hop

❝ In a place of immense poverty and oppression ▪ emerged this new urban form of expression

make Manhattan the center of wealth and business. During the 1950s, the city began construction of the massive Cross-Bronx Expressway to better connect the suburbs and make it easier to get to Manhattan. Carving through a densely populated urban neighborhood was no easy job. Historian Robert Caro writes, "The path of the great road lay across 113 streets,

avenues, and boulevards; sewers and water and utility mains numbering in the hundreds; one subway and three railroads; five elevated rapid transit lines, and seven other expressways or parkways."[1]

The seven-mile stretch of highway cut right through the heart of the borough and displaced over sixty thousand people. Robert Moses was the urban planner behind it all. In 1968, the completion of a 15,832 unit co-op apartment complex in the northern edge of the Bronx further accelerated the middle-class exodus from the Bronx. As Manhattan was renewed and cleaned up, the poorer African-American and Hispanic families were displaced to South Bronx. An aging neighborhood consisting mostly of lighter-skinned residents made a mass exit to Moses' newer and cleaner co-op neighborhoods, and to New Jersey and Long Island neighborhoods, which were now a much easier commute. And with all of the people leaving, several businesses and factories also fled. South Bronx lost most of its manufacturing jobs, and the average income dropped to less than half of the rest of the city.

Vacancy rates skyrocketed, and many reputable landlords sold out to slumlords. Several burned their buildings down in order to collect insurance money. With all of the budget cuts, the city ended up closing several fire stations in the Bronx. So with fewer firefighters and more fires, you can imagine the result. Most of these fires were not set because of riots or some major racial event. There was a different agenda. People left this wasteland behind and tried to profit however they could. Soon full blocks were burned out. Between 1973 and 1977, thirty thousand fires were set in the South Bronx, and more than forty-three thousand housing units were gone.

In 1973, New York governor Nelson Rockefeller put a new set of laws into effect that are still causing political unrest in New York. They became known as the Rockefeller drug reform laws. Some praised his reforms, but soon many more fought against them. The plan had a great purpose: to wipe out drug use in New York. But the ways of accomplishing it and funding it were seriously flawed. Rockefeller's plan included diverting funds from housing and public education into prison construction upstate. The laws also included serious penalties for anyone caught on the street with any amount of drugs. So instead of going after the suppliers and the ones profiting from the business, the laws targeted the street-level people using drugs or selling them in small quantities. Major drug traffickers usually escaped the sanctions of the Rockefeller drug laws, and prisons filled up faster than ever with serious sentences for nonviolent crimes. According to drugpolicy.org, "Research shows that drug use is relatively equal across categories of race and class, as well as across geographic region. And yet, nearly 92% of all those imprisoned under the Rockefeller Drug Laws are Black and Latino. Over 72% of all those imprisoned under the Rockefeller Drug Laws come from New York City."[2]

As the urban landscape changed, street gangs populated the deteriorating neighborhoods. Every teen and young adult was viewed as a gang member, even if they were just a regular kid. Places like the South Bronx experienced oppression under the laws being enforced by the state government. Activists are still fighting to reform these laws today.

THE GANG WARS

Each of us is made with the need to belong. Some people fulfill this need in fraternities, community organizations, or political groups. For others, it's street gangs. As I stated earlier, people in oppressed times band together

to find hope in something or someone. Many times, it's just about sur-
vival. In the South Bronx, thousands of teens and young adults found it in
gangs, which reemerged around 1968 and raged strong until about 1973.
These gangs weren't like the ones from the fifties and early sixties,

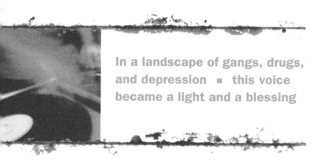

In a landscape of gangs, drugs, and depression ■ this voice became a light and a blessing

with their doo-wop music
and leather jackets. Growing up in crumbling terrain,
these rugged kids didn't
have much to care about.
Their gangs had names like
the Ghetto Brothers, Sav-
age Skulls, Roman Kings,
and the Black Spades.
West of the Bronx River,
the gangs were predominantly Puerto Rican, while east of the river they
were mostly African-American. The North Bronx also had some Italian
gangs. The gangs brought havoc to store owners, the elderly, drug addicts,
innocent youth, and each other. But many times they brought some order
to the neighborhood, since there was little police presence. Several of the
gangs would actually sweep out all the drug addicts and pushers. In 1972,
New York Post columnist Pete Hamill wrote, "The best single thing that
happened on the streets of New York in the past ten years is the re-
emergence of the teenage gangs ... these young people are standing up
for life, and if their courage lasts, they will help this city to survive."[3]

Although some positive things may have come out of the gangs at
times, eventually things got more violent and many lost their lives. At the
end of 1971, the gangs came to a major truce. Shortly after, NYPD's Bronx
Gang Task Force was formed. Soon many gang leaders ended up in jail,
and recruitment fell off as police cracked down everywhere. Other teens
grew up and got involved in different things. The gangs slowly disinte-
grated, and the next group of teens vibed to the new flavor—music.

OUT OF THE ASHES

Something rose from the ashes of the fires, the drug reform laws, the
unemployment, and the gangs. A new style of music that certain DJs were
throwing down at some block parties popped up around the Bronx. No one
would have ever guessed this would spark a whole new movement. The
style was originated by DJ Kool Herc. Originally from Kingston, Jamaica,
he brought a different twist to things, along with a huge sound system
that no one at the time could match. When he was DJing, he noticed that
the crowd got excited during the instrumental breakdown many songs had

in their rhythm section, so he invented a new technique that he called the merry-go-round. He took two copies of the same record, played the breakdown on one, and then switched to the other record also cued to the breakdown. While the second one played, he rewound the other one back to the breakdown and played it again. By repeating this process, a fifteen-second breakdown (also known as "the break") could be turned into a fifteen-minute breakdown, with the crowd going wild to their favorite parts. Soon nearly his entire routine focused on the breaks. Dancers competed during these times and even began to go down to the floor and incorporate some new moves. Many referred to them as the break boys, or the B-boys for short. Some argue that this is where the term *break dancing* came from. The term *B-boy* also meant Bronx Boy in many circles.

A new music had formed and a new dance had emerged, but what about the voice? At first, the DJ controlled the party and made some announcements, giving some shout-outs and trying to get the party excited. But as the breaks became the thing, the DJ was busy working the turntables like an instrument. Some DJs even added a third and fourth turntable to their routine to add some extra flavor. It became much too hectic to provide the music and also get on the mic. So DJs like Herc, Grandmaster Flash, and Afrika Bambaataa recruited others to join them and hype up the crowd. Shout-outs, chants, and short rhyming phrases grew into much more: these masters of ceremony quoting full verses and full songs that they had written. A new type of song and communication was

1973—the South Bronx was its dressing ∎ that clothed the culture's formation

birthed: rap. The movement now had a voice. Voices expressed the joy and pain of the inner city. The party that resided in apartments, rec centers, and gymnasiums moved outdoors where it could really grow. By the midseventies, the party had moved to the park. DJs took all their equipment and speakers with them, rigged up some electricity from a light post, and let the music rock. Soon these popular DJs moved with small armies of other DJs, rappers, and dancers.

THE ELEMENTS EMERGE

Hip-hop has four major elements or foundational components—DJing, MCing (rapping), breaking, and graffiti art. The first element, the DJ, brings the sound, the rhythm, and the music to shape the backdrop and set the atmosphere. As the turntables became an instrument, DJs pushed the creative boundaries even more. Grandmaster Flash studied how he could take mixing to the next level. Others began to experiment too, and a young cat named Theodore accidentally invented the scratch. Soon DJing became a performance as Flash developed a whole stage show in which he did tricks as he spun around and scratched with his elbows. It caught the crowd's attention, and soon many of the DJs learned these new styles to add to their own routines.

The second element, the MC or the rapper, became the voice of this new movement. Urban culture is very vocal, and the MC became that loud oral form of expression. Simple little old-school chants like "Throw your hands in the air and wave 'em like you just don't care" grew longer and became songs. Traveling with the DJs, these rappers formed their own groups, like the Furious Five, the L Brothers, and the Funky 4+1. As time went on, they grabbed more of the spotlight.

B-boying, widely known as break dancing, was the dance form of hip-hop. As the gang era faded out, it became a new way to battle with your crew and gain respect. Passionately and physically, you settled your beef on the floor rather than with your fists. The beginning styles were top-rocking or up-rocking, an aggressive dance style that took elements from martial arts and capoeira. But B-boy legend Crazy Legs claims, "Our immediate influence in B-boying was James Brown, point blank."[4] Eventually, the dance evolved and moved to the floor with floor footwork, spins, and freezes. Traveling from different neighborhoods, break-dancing crews challenged other crews to compete at the big block parties.

The final element was graffiti art, which became a way for this disenfranchised generation, which felt invisible, to be seen. As a graffiti writer named Futura 2000 says, "The name and the tag are one, that's what graffiti means; it's about identification, about a personal icon. It's a way of presenting yourself to the world, something like: Here I am!" This visual form of expression paved the way for urban youth to gain some instant street fame.

Graffiti writing has its roots in the 1960s in North Philadelphia. But it quickly spread to New York City and became part of the emerging culture in the Bronx. Many youth wrote their nickname along with their street number. A Greek-American graffiti writer, Taki 183, was the first to get his name in the *New York Times*. That was in 1971, when the art exploded. Simple tags turned into full aerosol "pieces," using full-color bubble letters with characters and style. Graffiti started in neighborhoods, with artists tagging abandoned buildings and signs. But it soon covered subway trains, making them moving billboards. Artists like Phase 2, Dondi, and Lady Pink covered the entire sides of twelve-foot by sixty-foot train cars. With the Bronx becoming a much more colorful place, graffiti art quickly spread to other boroughs as tagged trains traveled all through the city. By the early seventies, the city formed an antigraffiti task force, but they couldn't keep up with this growing phenomenon.

HIP-HOP WAS HERE

As you can see, this new movement created various forms of expression: music, vocal dialog, dance, and art. People from the outside could dispute its forms. But if you look closely, you'll see some incredibly creative people who started something from nothing. You'll see some people who practiced for countless hours maneuvering their turntables, writing songs, dancing, and doing their art. There was a new hope and purpose in these people's lives, a way to overcome oppression and poverty. Being part of something more constructive and fun, these youth and young adults tried to stay out of trouble and away from the fading gang scene. Not everything in the beginning of hip-hop was positive, but overall it was a creative, peaceful movement, not like what it has evolved to in today's mainstream culture.

But hip-hop was more than just the four elements. There was style, fashion, attitude, slang, street knowledge, beat-boxing, street entrepreneurship, and more. Even though people in the

Black and brown was the predominate original persuasion ■ for this gritty inner-city communication

Bronx may not have owned a nice house or even a car during the time this movement formed, people took more pride in the way they looked. There was a certain style in the way they laced up their sneakers and wore their hats or belts, elements of street fashion that still have an influence today. Style was closely interwoven with attitude and how you communicated, and there was a code for certain words, phrases, and knowledge. Beat-boxing came about when people made music with their mouths because they didn't have a sound system or a radio. Cats like Biz Markie, Doug E. Fresh, and the Fat Boys created this art form. Along with style and beat-boxing came hustling to make some money. Street entrepreneurship has always been part of life in the hood and was always a part of hip-hop. Some of the first block parties had people promoting the events on index cards and collecting a cover charge of a quarter or fifty cents, another example of trying to creatively make something out of nothing.

THE FIFTH ELEMENT: SPIRITUALITY IN EARLY HIP-HOP

Throughout history, every culture and every people group has some form of spirituality or faith. God created us with a longing to get to know him and to be connected. Many people get connected with false substitutes, but that doesn't invalidate their search. Hip-hop culture was no different. Even at the beginning of the movement, people searched for some higher purpose. Many consider the fifth element of hip-hop to be spirituality or knowledge of self. If you know the history of this culture, this truth is evident. But a few people have this aspect pretty twisted. This misinformed minority will tell people that hip-hop started from a false religion. Lacking knowledge of hip-hop's history, some members of the older generation focus on the negativity of today's mainstream hip-hop and jump on this bandwagon without knowing the facts.

New York City has always been a major portal into America, the place where most of the world wants to come to chase the American dream. Ever since the city formed, waves of immigrants have come there from all parts of the world, bringing their customs, cultures, and faiths with them. The South Bronx was predominately African-American and Latino, with many of its residents of color coming from Jamaica, Puerto Rico, and several other islands in the Caribbean. As a result, a wide variety of faiths are represented there—Christianity,

> It started rotating ∎ with DJ Kool Herc the Jamaican ∎ spinnin' breaks at the park—it was history in the makin'

Jehovah's Witnesses, Rastafarianism, Islam, Santeria, Five Percenters, and mixtures of these religions.

A noteworthy spiritual movement took place during the seventies. It didn't involve the majority, and it didn't become the foundation of or define the hip-hop movement, but it was definitely a part of the South Bronx in the 1970s. Bambaataa was a gang leader of the Black Spades in Bronx River Houses. He also was known as a popular DJ. He had a serious reputation and got respect everywhere he went. As the gang era faded, he got more into DJing. People still followed him everywhere he went. He started a peaceful organization in Bronx River as an alternative to the gangs.

In 1975, Bambaataa's cousin was shot and killed by police, which began a real change in his life. Instead of rallying everyone to fight back, he initiated peace. Bambaataa won an essay contest that year and took a trip to Africa and Europe. It opened his eyes. He saw black people living productive lives and running their cities. It inspired him to come back and start something new to stop the street violence and help his people elevate themselves. He changed his name to Afrika Bambaataa and began a new organization called the Zulu Nation, a peaceful organization with the motto "Peace, love, unity, and having fun."

From the beginning, the Zulu philosophy was very universal — to be open to all truth. They were down with both Allah and Jehovah, which is attractive to the postmodern mindset. (More on that in part 3.) But looking at their motto and their universalist attitude, you can see that this organization was really more about creating a peaceful, positive group to belong to than about some new religion or church.

By the early eighties, Bambaataa realized he needed to clarify what the Zulu Nation stood for. So he came out with the Infinity Lessons. Bam was known as an eclectic DJ who used all different styles of music. Many described his beliefs as eclectic as well. These lessons, drawing from the Nation of Islam, the Nation of Gods and Earths, and even the Black Panthers, were open-ended and constantly growing. In his book *Can't Stop, Won't Stop*, Jeff Chang states, "The Infinity Lessons seemed a quasi-theological mess, an autodidactic crazy quilt, a political road map to a nowhere. But to Bambaataa the ideas were less important than the process."[5] The Zulu Nation is still around today in some places, but very much in the background of mainstream hip-hop.

I had the opportunity to meet Bambaataa in 2004 when he visited Tampa to DJ a break-dancing event. Some of the breakers from my church knew him and told him about our church. He was intrigued and requested to meet me. I talked with Bam for about twenty minutes in the parking lot outside of a club. The negative things I heard about him from others didn't ring true. I found him to be a very humble, low-key guy. As I shared about our ministry and what Christ had done in my life, he listened intently. He commended us and seemed very open. Bam was excited to see that we were doing something positive for the culture by giving people hope and something to believe in. I gave him some Fla.vor Alliance CDs and a Fla.vor Fest DVD so he could hear and see what we are all about. Fla.vor Alliance is a record label I'm involved with that has a roster of artists based out of our church. Fla.vor Fest is an annual conference and music festival we hold each November at Crossover. When I gave him these products, his eyes lit up, and he reached into his glove compartment and pulled out a bootleg version of the Cross Movement's latest CD, along with a copy of Corey Red and Precise. He said, "I like this gospel rap stuff. I can play this on the college station I'm DJing for up in New York. I don't play all that garbage on mainstream radio. I need more of this stuff." My jaw dropped.

Here was the founder of Zulu Nation listening to Christian hip-hop, playing it on his station, and feeling it! Many may be disappointed that Christian hip-hop hasn't broken more ground, but it has planted more seeds than we'll ever know.

Throughout hip-hop history, a few spiritually minded figures have emerged. But we must keep in perspective that hip-hop is a culture of expression. Spirituality will always be a part of hip-hop and of American culture. Some of these people had strong leanings toward certain beliefs, which manifested in their lyrics and lifestyles. Although some may religiously follow hip-hop culture, it has never been a religion. Yes, there may be some groups that claim they are the religion of hip-hop, but it's just not factual. The masses in this culture don't follow a specific religion tied to hip-hop.

PERSONAL PERSPECTIVES FROM THE SOUTH BRONX

There are several books and countless websites that can give you a lot of information about hip-hop history, but there's nothing like hearing it directly from people who were there. Nearly half of my church is originally from New York City, and we have several people who grew up in the South Bronx as this culture was forming. Our youth pastor, Derrick Colon, performed a spoken-word piece on our *Cypha 5* CD describing what he saw growing up:

Up in the Bronx, from Tremont to Fordham, from Hoe Ave, to Creston, from Bronx River, the souls river would flow. Gangs were real way before the Warriors, death before dishonor was the motto, winos on the side of tenements sipping the bottle. Outlaws roaming the block, emcee boots stomping the block, the Savage Nomads, Chingalings, Savage Skulls locking the block. The South Bronx, burnt to a crisp, abandoned buildings would become the children's playground, across your ears you could hear the stray sound of bullets. This was as real as it gets, they tried to picture it by portraying the Sharks versus the Jets. No match, you had to live there to understand, and you can't grasp the feeling by reading a book, you had to be there. Grandmaster Melle Mel sent out the message to beware, "It's like a jungle sometimes it makes me wonder how I keep from going under." The thunder came from under the manholes where the iron horse roams to take people to their war-zoned homes. It was the Bronx of the seventies and eighties, where Bam was, the land was, Zulu, Five Percent, Ballbusters were relentless, Cold Crush 4, Fantastic 5, the Treacherous 3, emcee crews bringing the news that they were the best from the north to the south to the east to the west, yes, yes, ya'll you don't stop, yo hip-hop, Jesus is the rock! Rock on!

Derrick recently wrote a screenplay with our drama director called *To Hip-Hop, with Love*, in which he shares what unfolded before his eyes. Our ministry hosted this production several times, and it resulted in many people building new relationships with Christ. It has also been developed into a book that is a great resource.

B-boys hit the floor with titles for the takin' ■ MCs spit their art from the heart and not for the bacon

DJ Flame, formerly known as DJ Spank, is a female Christian DJ who performs at several events around NYC, writes for several publications, and leads the NYC chapter of the Urban Gospel Alliance. She was part of a pioneer female DJ crew called Mercedes Ladies and grew up in the Bronx in the seventies. She says,

> I believe God allowed hip-hop to emerge back in the day to be an outlet to the frustrated, the downtrodden, and the underdog. Minorities didn't have a voice back then. But this was a way to communicate; this was a way we could escape. I had a voice ... through my turntables I would speak a language that only a select few would understand. Those street gangs that were killing each other started attending outdoor jams, and slowly but surely, they started putting the guns down. They started break dancing, DJing, and MCing. Some couldn't do anything regarding the art form, so they became security. So much good came out of hip-hop then. It was nothing like now. People even wanted to go back to school so they could better learn how to write so they could be a better MC.[6]

Corey Red is another Christian hip-hop artist who grew up in the South Bronx in the seventies. His gritty inner-city experiences have shaped him into the minister he is today. Spending time with him, I've heard him express many times how much hip-hop has changed for the worse since its early days.

HIP-HOP SPILLS OUT OF THE BRONX

In the late seventies, the culture spilled out of the Bronx into the other boroughs. Kids in Queens, Manhattan, and Brooklyn imitated their Bronx counterparts. But what propelled hip-hop music to the world outside the Bronx was its first-ever recording on a vinyl record. Several rap groups were approached by different record labels to record the first rap song and make it available to the public. Some groups were skeptical. Ironically, the first group to do it wasn't even known for rocking jams in the parks or in the local clubs. They were just some fellas from within the culture who stepped up to some people from outside the culture and said they could make a record. Many of their phrases and rhymes were copied from established groups. Nonetheless, in the fall of 1979, the Sugarhill Gang released the first hip-hop twelve-inch vinyl single, *Rapper's Delight*. It changed history.

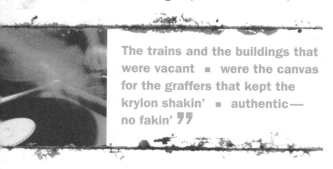

The trains and the buildings that were vacant ■ were the canvas for the graffers that kept the krylon shakin' ■ authentic— no fakin' "

The song spread across New York City and hit black radio. It soon popped up on the national Top 40. *Rapper's Delight* even spread overseas, becoming the bestselling twelve-inch single ever pressed. At one point, the record sold around seventy-five thousand copies a week. *Rapper's Delight* was not only the first hip-hop record; it became the first hip-hop record to sell platinum. (Over one million copies!) With disco fading out and several record labels struggling, suddenly the potential of this new music had the attention of label executives, radio, and media—and, of course, the original groups, who had never imagined it could get this big.

6 Crossing Over into the Mainstream

People wondered if *Rapper's Delight* was just a one-time hit, a quickly passing fad. They found out that it wasn't. A national audience was ready for more of this new kind of music. Just months after the surprise success of *Rapper's Delight*, Kurtis Blow became the first major-label rap artist when he signed with Mercury Records. He soon released the platinum-selling *Christmas Rappin'* and *The Breaks*. Around the same time, Flash and the Furious Five signed a deal and released *Superappin'*.

Everything began to change as the rapper became the center of attention and a hot commodity. Hip-hop was all about a block party run by the DJ: songs that went on and on as rappers just kept flowing and breakers did their thing on the floor. It was an experience that didn't fit into a three-minute and thirty-second radio slot. *Rapper's Delight* was over fifteen minutes long, and people who knew the culture were astonished that they cut it that short! Now label execs and radio people tried to get groups to cut their songs down so they would fit into the radio format. Many consider this the death of old-school hip-hop. The DJ was soon cut out of the picture and all of the focus was on the rappers. Even at block parties and clubs, the focus shifted to the rappers as they stepped up their talent and became the loudest element.

Although the movement was a form of expression, most of the lyrical content centered on having a good time and rappers' building their reputations. As records went national and even international, some artists realized they had a platform from which to speak. In 1981, Grandmaster Flash and the Furious Five put out a record called *The Message*, the title track of which is said to be hip-hop's first political form of expression. It's a vivid description of the conditions in the ghetto, a socially conscious song that told of the reality of inner-city life. This track paved the way for rhymes that included politics and social justice. Suddenly hip-hop wasn't just party music. It became music that made you think. During the 1980s, artists expressed themselves and talked about all kinds of different topics.

BREAK DANCING SWEEPS THE PLANET!

By the early eighties, break dancing had died down in the South Bronx neighborhoods where it originated. But it soon crossed over into the mainstream with the help of some movies. The 1983 movie *Flashdance* featured break dancing from some of the Rock Steady Crew. It caught the attention of filmmakers, and *Breakin'* and *Beat Street* were released in the summer of 1984. *Breakdance* provides some of my earliest memories of hip-hop. I had heard some rap music years before and thought it was cool, but the breakin' (slang for break dancing) captured me. Everyone at

> 66 It didn't take long for people to start to bite ■ if you know your history the classic example is *Rapper's Delight* ■ the genre's first national record with half the lyrics the rappers didn't (even) write

my school was soon breakin' every single chance we got. The phenomenon swept the country and beyond. Breakin' was featured at the 1984 Olympics and in a McDonald's commercial. But with several more movies and marketing overkill in just over a year, breakin' became another fad. When I talk to people who were in school during that time, they remember how big breakin' was, no matter where they were from. Anyone alive then can remember seeing it everywhere for a brief time period. Although it quickly faded out of the limelight, breakin' went underground and eventually reemerged with dancers taking the moves to a seemingly impossible higher level.

THE REAL CROSSOVER BEGINS

Even though there had been a few platinum and gold records, skepticism of this new music remained. Many were still convinced that it would soon fade out. None of the artists ever had a solid deal with real marketing and real push—until Run-D.M.C. The group's manager, Russell Simmons, who was also the older brother of group-member Run, proudly stated, "Run-D.M.C. is the most important act in hip-hop history."[7] They signed with Profile Records, an independent label. Their first album went gold and caught the attention of some important people. Russell hustled and partnered with Rick Ruben to start a label named Def Jam. They soon became the first indie hip-hop label to go major, signing a million-dollar deal with Columbia. They signed a young kid named LL Cool J and a trio of white rappers who called themselves the Beastie Boys. Now people from the culture were influencing and running a part of the industry, taking hip-hop to a whole new platform.

Run-D.M.C. was the first rap group to be on MTV. Their single "Rock Box" was rock-influenced and tapped into a whole new audience of young white Americans who followed this new music channel. As the national audience grew, there were major national tours with hip-hop groups packing out major arenas. By 1986, Run-D.M.C.'s third album came out and sold millions. They hit the road with a sixty-four-date tour and eventually joined with LL Cool J, the Beastie Boys, and Whodini. LL and the Beasties also enjoyed platinum success. By 1987, there was no denying that hip-hop had crossed over, and the myth that it was a fad faded.

VARIOUS THEMES

Hip-hop's early lyrics focused on having a good time. During the eighties, most crossover groups maintained this flavor, writing lyrics which were clean compared with the mainstream hip-hop you hear today. As one website says, "Do you recall when rap was actually fun and creative, rather than vulgar, violent and generic? If you do, then you were a child of the eighties."[8] I personally recall this time. During the eighties, I was in junior high and high school. Many people consider this time and the early nineties to be the golden era of hip-hop. Many true lyricists emerged on the scene and took hip-hop to the next level.

A little while back, I attended a break-dancing event in Orlando that was held by Skill Methodz, a popular B-boy crew in the current world of breakin'. Most of the crew members used to live in Tampa and would attend Crossover and dance after service. Since then, many have moved on to New York and LA to be in movies, commercials, shows, videos, and tours. They are some incredibly talented individuals. Several of them built relationships with God for the first time as they attended our ministry. (Keep these brothers in your prayers, since they have a lot of distractions around them at times.) I bring this event up because all the music being played was from the late eighties and some early nineties, even though it was November 2005. I remember looking around the room and observing more than two hundred breakers from all over the world getting down like it was 1988. The skill was incredible, as the speed, footwork, and power moves have taken on whole new dimensions. But in the middle of watching all these great urban acrobatic moves, I heard the artists of my teenage years—cats with some serious rhymes, like Big Daddy Kane, Eric B. and Rakim, and Public Enemy (or PE). The flows and the music still sounded up to date and honestly were much better than most of what's out there in the mainstream now.

It ain't right ▪ but platinum sales propelled the culture worldwide overnight ▪ now the spotlight ▪ was in hip-hop's corner

A lot of hip-hop groups you heard on the radio had positive messages that made you think. KRS-One and Boogie Down Productions produced several socially conscious songs promoting education and family. A song that really stood out in my mind is "Love's Gonna Get Cha." KRS told the story about a kid from the ghetto who had nothing and eventually started selling drugs to get by. Soon the love for money took over and he became a major dealer. His life fell apart when he committed murder and got jail time. It was a powerful song that made my crew and me think. While movies and the streets said this stuff was cool, here was an artist who said, "No, it's not cool. Here's the truth about it." Parents, coaches, and schoolteachers said the same message, but many took it to heart when they heard hip-hop artists say it. We listened because of the platform they had, because of their packaging and their ability to communicate. It was the first song I heard that really rocked me and showed me that hip-hop can deliver a strong positive message. Unfortunately, some artists who put out positive songs still had negative songs, which made them seem to be contradicting themselves.

Artists like Eric B. and Rakim hit the scene, introducing the art form of sampling. Run-D.M.C. had stripped their music down to beat machines and bass lines with a little guitar thrown in. Eric B. and Rakim further re-structured the soundscape by using creatively sampled loops from artists like James Brown. Soon other artists sampled and remade funk and R&B songs from back in the day. As music producers sampled, cut, snipped, and filtered old songs, it became the new standard for laying down tracks. Some people from older generations said this was destroying old songs and the original artist's credibility, but in reality, it brought many of these older hits back into the spotlight and breathed a breath of fresh air into some of these artists' careers.

POLITICAL RAP

Although the typical theme of hip-hop in the eighties was having a good time, some groups focused on a socially conscious message. One group took this a step farther into the political arena. Although the culture was still centered in New York City, the influential group Public Enemy hailed from the suburbs of Long Island. And they were different: militant, pro-black, and serious. The group signed with Def Jam Records, and their leader, Chuck D., soon began to ruffle quite a few feathers. He went after everyone, from the government to black radio. In an interview with Harry Allen of *BRE* (*Black Renaissance Exclusive*), Chuck D. stated, "Whether or not radio plays us, millions of people listen to rap because rap is America's TV station. Rap gives you all the news on all phases of life, good and bad, pretty and ugly, drugs, sex, education, love, money, war, peace—you name it."[9] Chuck was raised by his mother, who embraced the Black Panther movement and other civil rights organizations. So he had politics in his blood, and he had a beef with the system and how it treated his people.

But soon the DJ, the graff artist, and the breaker were a goner
- cuz they only could market the MC into the radio format
- soon the other elements got stepped on like a doormat

Although Public Enemy was loud, militant, and clearly pro-black, the funny thing is that more than half of their fans weren't black. I know this to be true because I was a huge Public Enemy fan. They were *the* group in my high school in New Jersey in 1988 and 1989. My high school was comprised mostly of minorities, but a lot of Hispanics and white kids loved PE just as much as the black kids. There was something about the energy and authority of their music. A big part of their appeal was their rebellion against the system. Youth culture always loves that, whatever the genre of music. But Public Enemy spoke a lot of truth about what was going on in

America at that time. It was undeniable that a lot of what they expressed was true. Chuck D. proclaimed that rap music was now black America's CNN. In actuality, it became the multicultural hip-hop generation's CNN.

1983—yo, let's explore that ■ Run-D.M.C. landed a deal with a major label ■ MTV launched and now America could catch MCs on cable

Even though PE was serious and the music was driving, they had one member who lightened it up and made it fun to listen to and watch. His name was Flavor Flav, the crazy hype man who wore the huge clock. Even though PE faded in popularity during the nineties, Flavor Flav has made a huge comeback the past few years through several celebrity reality TV shows on VH1, reinforcing PE's true mainstream appeal.

YO! MTV RAPS

One of my favorite pastimes as a teenager was checking out *Yo! MTV Raps* every day at 4:30. My family didn't have cable. But my friend across the street did, so every day after school I'd head over to his crib. *Yo! MTV Raps* was a music video show featuring all the latest rap songs. It was one of the major influences that brought hip-hop into the mainstream. Most people in my neighborhood didn't watch any of the rock music videos on MTV, but we would check the network out to see if they'd pop in a rap video. *Yo! MTV Raps* dedicated an entire hour to rap videos only, giving us a way to connect with the artists we were listening to. We not only heard them but saw what they looked like, how they dressed, and often where they were from. The show soon became the highest-rated show on the network, as rap music was exploding. The *Los Angeles Times* stated, "Within a year, MTV had gone from almost no rap programming to twelve hours of rap programming."[10] The hosts, Fab 5 Freddy, Dr. Dre, and Ed Lover, would cut up, have a good time, and introduce the latest videos. The show was one of the biggest vehicles that took hip-hop out of the inner cities and into the suburbs and beyond.

THE BIRTH OF GANGSTA RAP

As 1990 approached, the themes and boundaries of rap expanded. It had been around and experienced some great crossover hits for several years. So what was next? Artists and record labels looked at how they could stand out from the rest. This is where hip-hop took a turn for the worse. Several rap groups came out of Los Angeles in the 1980s, but none of them made it nationally. Many of the groups imitated East Coast groups from the hip-hop mecca of NYC. Even people from the West Coast really didn't take their own artists seriously. LA looked for its own sound, trying to find a way to stand out and represent the Left Coast.

In 1987, a struggling producer named Dr. Dre found himself producing tracks for a new label called Ruthless after they paid his bail. A studio session with one of the artists went sour, so Dre pushed the owner of the label, Eazy-E, into the sound booth and had him record something so that the studio time wasn't wasted. That night a new artist was born who sparked a new style of destructive rap from the West Coast. Eazy-E and his group of gangsta-style rappers became known as N.W.A. (Niggaz with Attitude). Gangs, which were still a big thing in California, became a major theme of N.W.A.'s rhymes and storytelling. When their album *N.W.A. and the Posse* hit the streets later that year, it became popular because people identified with it. Suddenly, the West Coast now had an identity, and they ran with it.

Even though *N.W.A. and the Posse* found a lot of success at the street level, no major labels wanted to touch it at first because it was too violent and vulgar. But eventually a new label, Priority Records, signed N.W.A. and rereleased *N.W.A. and the Posse*. With a limited budget and no radio play, it still sold over 300,000 copies. In 1988, Eazy-E put out a solo album that quickly went gold. The record company realized they were onto something, so they encouraged N.W.A. to really push the envelope on their next album. Dr. Dre bragged in an interview about "wanting to go all the way left." He shared how everyone was doing the Black Power thing, so they were going to give them an alternative filled with profanity, leaving nothing to the imagination. These guys were going right to it—violence, sex, crime.

> Eric B. and Rakim, P.E., B.D.P. showed that hip-hop was stable ■ and not a passing trend ■ for many it was true love, not a passing friend

When the new album, *Straight Outta Compton*, dropped in early 1988, it took off. It sold over two million copies. Why? Humans love sin. Movies, TV, and magazines supplied a lot of vulgar and profane stuff, but putting it in music, a form that could be consumed on the streets, was a new angle. The controversial material had a big shock factor, and people ate it up. The album also brought about a big change in hip-hop. Up to this point,

New York City was the center of the culture. By coming out and representing Compton to the fullest, N.W.A. made it cool to represent wherever you were from. Everyone had a story to tell, from Atlanta to Chicago to London to Tokyo.

The same year, a group from Miami called 2 Live Crew broke into the mainstream with their album *As Nasty as They Wanna Be*. They weren't considered gangsta rap, but they were definitely in the shock rap category. The group took sexual content to a level never seen in music before. It was basically a hip-hop porn album. As it hit the mainstream, complaints poured in from several organizations, such as the American Family Association. The group got arrested several times on their tour for performing lewd acts on stage during their concerts.

In June 1990, the album was banned in Florida by Judge Jose Gonzalez, and several record store owners were arrested for selling it. I remember seeing stories in the news almost every day for several months. Several additional court cases attempted to ban the album. They even put a parental guidance sticker on it, and you couldn't buy it if you were under seventeen, which caused quite a ruckus. People who didn't even like 2 Live Crew's music argued for their constitutional right to say what they wanted. It got ugly.

You might have thought this was bad publicity for the group. But in reality, it was great. More controversy plus more curiosity equaled more album sales. Throwing the sticker on it only made it more desirable for teens. The album sold millions. A friend of mine bought it, and I remember borrowing it to check it out. Even though I wasn't living a Christian life at the time, I was still shocked and offended. I couldn't believe people would say this stuff on an album. It degraded women terribly; I felt bad for them and embarrassed that other guys acted like that. Unfortunately, it ushered hip-hop into an anything-goes era in which women were more and more disrespected. Record labels encouraged and even pressured artists to add more profanity because of its sales potential. The A and R representatives from the labels gave more input and shaped the artists, knowing that poison would sell.

"SELF-DESTRUCTION"

When you feed people poison, they eventually get sick. It's not all the music's fault. It's a combination of things—society, family situations, schooling, movies, TV, and, yes, the music. These things help shape people's worldview and their behavior. Conditions during the late eighties in urban neighborhoods and in urban families deteriorated along with the morals in rap music. The media spotlighted the escalating violence tied to the culture. There were several murders at rap concerts in LA, Nashville, Connecticut, and NYC. Rap wasn't the only music genre associated with violence, but it was at the forefront because it was a new urban thing with a real edge. Hip-hop began to get a bad reputation, and it seemed like things began to self-destruct.

The Stop the Violence movement formed to put out a benefit record, a video, and a book. The group planned to rally the culture around the motto "Stop the violence" and brought together an all-star lineup of East Coast rappers to record the song and video "Self-Destruction." The track quickly became the hottest thing for several months. Even though the song was pretty long, it kept our attention with many flavors from different rappers. Most of the words from that classic cut preached positive messages and empowerment. I can still remember many of the lyrics. It was a great moment in hip-hop, but it didn't go down like we thought. There were artists who were concerned about the state of the culture

> But the industry wanted the envelope to push and bend ■ soon the original identity was about to end "

and their communities, but it was the publicists, A and R reps, and label execs who put the campaign together. They brought everyone together to shift the negative media coverage and show there were good, responsible things coming out of hip-hop. It worked. The heat was off the industry, but unfortunately, the Stop the Violence movement quickly faded away.

7 The New Pop Culture

By the early 1990s, hip-hop had crept more into pop culture. Movies like *Boyz N the Hood*, *New Jack City*, and *Juice* were the first to portray current life in the inner city. These blockbuster films did very well because they got national theater distribution, proving there was a serious fan base for hip-hop-influenced movies. And with the huge numbers they pulled, it was obvious that the audience was bigger than the urban audience. People from the suburbs checked these movies out, just like they were buying the albums.

Even though gangsta rap took a lot of the spotlight in the early nineties, some cleaner rap took the pop charts by storm. A California rapper named MC Hammer came out with "U Can't Touch This," a remake of the Rick James song "Super Freak." Known for his incredible dance moves and his super-baggy pants, Hammer toured the country and beyond with his huge entourage of dancers. Gangsta rap made its mark in the streets, but Hammer's rap was safe for radio and video. He even had some credibility in the hood in the beginning of his career because of his dancing talent. When I was in high school, everyone imitated the new Hammer dance moves and rocked his signature pants. Hammer's album broke all previous records and became the biggest-selling hip-hop album to date, selling more than eleven million copies.

Another artist who fit this category was Vanilla Ice. He toured with Hammer and also had the dance moves and the flashy style. The thing about Ice was that he was white. The white audience briefly had someone to connect with in hip-hop who seemed credible and had flavor. But author James Haskins exposed Ice, writing, "He said that he had grown up knowing hardship, attending a tough, inner-city Miami high school as a classmate of Luther Campbell of 2 Live Crew, and that he had been stabbed in a gang fight."[11] Apparently, he used all of this to gain credibility in the black-dominated world of rappers. For a short time, he gained a lot of fans and sold several million albums with his hit "Ice Ice Baby." But as his stardom increased, some journalists found out that he grew up in middle-class suburban

Hip-Hop

66 The '90s ushered in the gangsta-rap era ■ this soon became a major rap error

Texas. Once this news hit the streets, Vanilla Ice looked like a joke, and his career was instantly ruined. In the hip-hop world, he was a classic example of the one-hit wonder.

In 1991, *Billboard* magazine switched its weekly charts to a new program called SoundScan, which used bar codes and a point-of-purchase system to track actual sales of records. Before then, all the different charts were based on a network of retail reports that weren't accurate. Tommy Boy owner Tom Silverman was an early advocate of SoundScan, pointing out that no one knew what criteria *Billboard* used to chart their Top 20. Several hip-hop albums sold hundreds of thousands of copies but never saw the charts, or only saw the fringes of it. When *Billboard* first released the official numbers with their new charting system, it shocked the industry. Pop and rock albums didn't rule the charts as they had for years. The niche markets of country, metal, and rap were the movers and shakers. Country had its established market, and metal had already peaked, but rap had just begun its crossover to the mainstream, so its potential was huge.

HIP-HOP IN PRINT

The hip-hop culture had a voice in the media through the music and through videos played on MTV, but there hadn't really been anything in print. Of course, countless people wrote about it in many different publications like *Billboard*, the *Village Voice*, and even *Rolling Stone*. But they were people from the outside looking in. This loosely knit emerging culture didn't have a publication that reported extensively about itself. By the late eighties, there were some hip-hop newsletters being published by a few different people around the country. One publication, run by a multicultural group of young educated guys who were passionately involved in hip-hop, emerged as the authority by 1990. Their new magazine, called *The Source*, first started out as a rap industry trade magazine with a lot of regional reporting. Yet as they grew, their focus became more national, and they changed their masthead to read, "The magazine of hip-hop music, culture and politics." The magazine covered artists, news, and fashion, and included editorials and the sacred five-mic rating guide for record reviews. In *Advertising Age*, Janice Kelly wrote, "In 1991 after their move to New York, *The Source* had a circulation of 40,000, captured 286 ad pages between $2,000 to $3,000 a page, and was clocking nearly a million in total revenues."[12] It seemed like an overnight success, but it was just the beginning. By the end of the nineties, *The Source* had increased its circulation to five hundred thousand, with more than thirty million dollars in revenue. It outsold even *Rolling Stone* magazine, showing how big the culture's influence had become.

Several other magazines popped up as people wanted a piece of this growing market. In 1992, Time-Warner got in on it and started a more commercial hip-hop magazine called *Vibe*. Advertising executives wondered if two major hip-hop magazines could exist in this smaller niche market. A year later, they realized that it was much bigger than any of them had thought. Other smaller magazines like *Rap Pages* and *URB* also hit the scene. The competition only expanded the market, and major companies like Tommy Hilfiger, Timberland, Nike, the Gap, and Sprite wanted in on hip-hop's newfound influence. Corporate giants like AT&T, Sony, and even the U.S. Army took out ads.

Along the way, several other magazines emerged, including *Blaze*, *Elemental*, and *XXL*. Many others came and went, but today there are more hip-hop magazines than ever. And the competition at the top is fierce. The top two, *The Source* and *XXL*, have carried on a constant battle of editorials, hype, and gossip. Some in the culture have turned their backs on these magazines, complaining that they have changed and become too corporate and commercialized. Much of this is true. But one thing for sure is that these magazines have become consumer catalogs to the hip-hop lifestyle, and people religiously read them.

THE MELTDOWN

By the midnineties, hip-hop expanded its influence in many new ventures and partnerships. People got rich off it, and more greed crept in. In the beginning, it was about a love for the art and the culture. People wanted to express themselves and loved their artistry. They would be in hip-hop no matter what. But eventually it was all about the money. The mentality changed fast as hip-hop became more commercialized. Many hip-hop artists were now simply actors, in it to get paid. A and R representatives scouted for artists who had a certain look,

Cuz now cats was making more bread than Panera ▪ and their rhymes was leaving more blood-stains than marinara

reshaping them to make the label a lot of money. With ghetto superstar dreams, many of these artists signed their lives away for their new job. For many, it became just that—a job, all about following a formula for what would sell. Some things have changed since this meltdown, but unfortunately this mentality is still alive and well in hip-hop today. Many just want to make money and don't care how it affects anyone else. They don't take responsibility for their lyrics or their lifestyle.

Things got out of control. The gangsta-rap era of the early nineties affected not only its listeners but also the artists and the people running the industry. Situations at *The Source* magazine led to physical violence, and the entire editorial staff resigned. At the second annual Source Music Awards, Suge Knight of Death Row Records from the West Coast stepped up to the podium and called out Puff Daddy (now known as Diddy) and his East Coast record label, Bad Boy. A beef had emerged between their two main artists, Tupac Shakur (Death Row) and Biggie Smalls (Bad Boy). The media quickly hyped this as an all-out East Coast versus West Coast thing. People everywhere talked about it in the barbershop, at school, and on the street corner. Hip-hop culture seemed to be in the middle of the biggest fight in its history. Many artists bragged about how much dirt they did and how hard they were. Reputations were at stake. More important, money was at stake. An escalation of violence was bound to happen. The masses would follow whoever won the battle.

On September 7, 1996, Tupac and Death Row Records owner Suge Knight were driving to a nightclub on East Flamingo Road in Las Vegas. They were in town to watch the Mike Tyson–Bruce Seldon heavyweight championship boxing match. Tyson was supposed to meet up with them later at Club 662, where Tupac was scheduled to perform. But Tupac never made it. A Cadillac pulled alongside Knight's rented BMW 750, and a gunman in the back seat opened fire on the passenger side of the car. Tupac was hit three times. Six days later, he died in the hospital. He was only twenty-five. The rumor was that Biggie and Bad Boy were behind the shooting, but police could find no solid suspects. Six months later, Tupac's East Coast rival Biggie Smalls was shot dead by a gunman on March 9 as he left a *Vibe* magazine party in Los Angeles. He was only twenty-four.

This was a sobering time in the history of hip-hop. Many people woke up and realized things needed to change. Several artists produced tributes, filled with spiritual overtones, to these deceased icons. Fans also paid tribute, and album sales went through the roof. Shortly after Tupac's death, a collection of his music was released under the alias Makaveli, titled *The Don Killuminati: The 7 Day Theory*. The name Makaveli came from sixteenth-century Italian philosopher Machiavelli, who apparently faked his own death to gain power. This created even more controversy and questions. Was Tupac really dead? Rumors floated around the internet, leading millions to believe he wasn't, further fueling album sales. *Newsweek* reported that Tupac's albums have grossed more than forty million dollars since his death. Tupac also appeared in several movies following his death, which helped keep his image alive.

Bulging egos, bulging stress ▪ then this bulging beef between the east and the west ▪ blown up by the press

He actually became number eight in *Forbes* magazine's list of the richest deceased celebrities.

Interestingly enough, Biggie Smalls' album prior to his death was titled *Ready to Die*. The album that released just after his death was named *Life after Death* and sold more than ten million copies. Death had become a commodity, and the industry cashed in on it. Several conspiracy theories even popped up saying that the record labels had the artists killed because they knew it would increase album sales, making them better assets dead than alive.

At this time, a shift in the culture was noticeable. The culture now thought about the afterlife, responsibility, and change. But it wasn't long before people forgot. Our Western culture is moved by tragedies like 9-11, the tsunami, and Hurricane Katrina, but we quickly return to our daily routines. Our main problem is that we don't learn from our mistakes, so we end up repeating history again and again. Although these deaths in hip-hop are the most remembered, there have been several others since. As I'm writing this book, there is a huge beef between East Coast rapper 50 Cent and West Coast rapper the Game. Once again things are getting out of hand, with many industry insiders speculating that this could be another big East Coast versus West Coast battle.

MEDIA CONSOLIDATION

In 1996, Congress passed the Telecommunications Act. This new law deregulated radio. There were no longer any ownership caps. In the wake of the resulting consolidation of radio stations, the airwaves were dominated by only a few corporate giants—Clear Channel, Viacom, Cumulus, and Citadel. Privately owned FM stations claimed they would never sell out to the majors, but when the big boys came and offered several million more than their stations were worth, they took the offers. After overpaying for the stations, these majors laid off hundreds of employees, took away

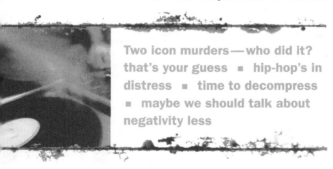

Two icon murders—who did it? that's your guess ■ hip-hop's in distress ■ time to decompress ■ maybe we should talk about negativity less

community programming, and standardized playlists across the country. Clear Channel went from forty stations in 1996 to 1,240 stations by 2003.

The new monopolies had several effects. First, many stations lost their DJs, who were local heroes. It became nearly impossible for local or independent artists to get any airplay, since the playlists were controlled by some corporate office in some other city. Second, there were format changes in many cities. Corporations understood the global demand for post-white pop culture. They realized hip-hop was the next big thing and that younger generations were looking more and more to minorities as their heroes in sports, movies, and music.

Hip-hop already had its hold on large urban cities, since many of them had a few stations playing hip-hop all the time. When I was growing up in Philly, we had three stations playing hip-hop all the time. When I first moved to Tampa in 1996, there was no FM hip-hop station. The Top

40 station played maybe 30 percent urban music, which included some hip-hop, but the only station that had daily hip-hop programming was an AM station with sketchy reception. In 1999, Clear Channel started an FM station that played hip-hop twenty-four hours a day. Their DJs were two corny white surfer guys who were supposedly broadcasting from their dad's stolen boat out in the gulf. True hip-hop listeners thought this was weak, but they listened because now they had a radio station that played their music. Of course, all the suburban kids connected with these surfer DJs, creating a bridge from their culture to the music. It was marketing genius. The station was an overnight success and became the number-one Arbitron-rated station in the area.

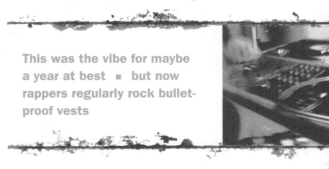

This was the vibe for maybe a year at best ∎ but now rappers regularly rock bulletproof vests

Suddenly, there were noticeable changes in youth and young-adult culture. Within a year, the malls had several new hip-hop clothing stores. And everywhere you went, hip-hop was the identity of the younger generations in this smaller emerging city. In 2004, a second FM hip-hop station was added, and the music the Top 40 station played was close to 80 percent urban.

In his book *The Media Monopoly*, Ben Bagdikian writes, "By then [late nineties], just ten companies controlled most of the U.S. media landscape—down from fifty in 1983—including music, movies, magazines, television, video games, and the Internet."[13] Most people also didn't realize that Viacom soon owned both MTV and BET (Black Entertainment Television). Even BET was no longer black owned. Chuck D. from Public Enemy broke down the reality about the people who now controlled hip-hop: "You got five corporations that control retail. You got four who are the dominant record labels. Then you got three radio outlets who own all the stations. You got two television networks and you got one video outlet. I call it 5-4-3-2-1. Boom!"[14] This consolidation has stifled creativity and diversity. Everything has become packaged and commercialized, with fewer voices, opinions, news sources, and innovative art available to the public. It's really scary to think that such a small percentage controls everything we watch, listen to, and read! That's some serious power. Unfortunately, most of the people in power in the media don't have a relationship with Christ, so the worldview we get is often twisted.

THE NEW ECONOMY

Now that hip-hop was a hot commodity, media monopolies were looking not just for a hit song but for a whole line of products and goods to accompany the song. Russell Simmons, founder of Def Jam Records, became a key player in getting corporate America to use hip-hop to sell their products. His company, Rush Communications, has worked with Coke, ESPN, HBO, Estée Lauder, and Tommy Hilfiger, and Simmons founded Phat Farm clothing in the early nineties. Although business was slow in the beginning, it soon took off. Clothing lines became the new craze among artists. Today, nearly every major hip-hop artist has a clothing line or is about to launch one. P. Diddy started Sean Jean, Eminem started Shady, 50 Cent started G-Unit, Jay-Z started Rocawear, and the list goes on and on. Along with these clothing lines, there are sneakers, video games, energy drinks, rims, and even high-end liquor. Ten years ago, most malls may have had one store that carried some hip-hop clothing or specialized in it. But today most malls in metropolitan areas have several stores that carry only these clothing lines. In addition, every major department store carries many of these brands and others, like Ecko and Akademiks, as the centerpiece of their young men's department. You can also walk into most athletic footwear stores like Foot Locker, Champs, and Athlete's Foot and also find all of these brands on display. These clothing lines have become the bread and butter for many artists, and several of them bring in annual sales of more than one hundred million dollars.

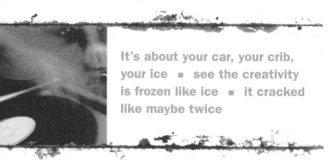

It's about your car, your crib, your ice ■ see the creativity is frozen like ice ■ it cracked like maybe twice

On February 18, 2004, an article on Forbes.com stated,

> When hip-hop was young, big business was put off by the violence and the controversy associated with the music. Now, there's no difference between investing in a hip-hop artist and investing in Celine Dion, says Morris Reid, managing director of youth marketing consultancy Blue Fusion. "It's all business; you have to take a risk either way," he adds. Not only is corporate America now taking the genre seriously, but so are investors ... So now we have the Sean John Lincoln Navigator by Ford, the Jay-Z athletic shoe by Reebok and Pimp Juice, an energy drink by Nelly. Where does it all

end? "Hip-hop is like water . . . There's nothing you can do to stop it."[15]

The urban form of expression that started in the ghettos of New York City has emerged as a ten-billion-dollars-a-year industry.

This new economy brought an indulgence mentality to the hip-hop community, which really reflects American culture as a whole. Luxury is in. Saving money and investing for the future are out. Everyone lives for the moment and beyond their means. For the first time in American history, our country spends more than it makes, which will bring some serious repercussions down the road. Hip-hop is on the forefront of this material-istic bandwagon. If you tune in the music channels and check out a music video, you'll notice the emphasis on stuff: luxury cars, huge rims, man-sions, diamonds, the finest clothes. Shows like *MTV Cribs* or VH1's *The Fabulous Lifestyle of . . .* have the masses lusting for more. And because hip-hop sprang from a low-income environment, it has always reflected the desire to have these things. When a luxurious lifestyle became a reality for many artists, their spending went through the roof.

In 2005, Minya Oh published a book titled *Bling Bling: Hip Hop's Crown Jewels*, which is filled with pictures and stories documenting the jewelry and diamonds that different artists have worn throughout hip-hop history. Many of us can remember the 1980s, when artists wore thick gold chains. Those five- to ten-thousand-dollar chains now look like something you'd get in a gumball machine compared with what the hottest artists wear today. Customized jewels are in,

> It's obvious their content is stuck in a vice ■ but they making money, who needs advice?

making even the artists' jewelers into celebrities. In the hip-hop world, Jacob the Jeweler in New York is the go-to guy. Artists have dropped over a million dollars with him for different custom diamond pieces.

Some of the top artists truly are making millions, but there are many upcoming artists who are only acting like they have made it. Many music videos today are filled with rented props. Very few of the artists really own that stuff. The Bentley is rented, along with the mansion, the girls by the pool, and the jewelry. It's all fake! But youth and young adults are sucked into thinking this is what it's all about, when in reality, very few are liv-ing that lifestyle. And if you've heard some of the interviews with the top stars, they say they still haven't found happiness. Yet seeing all they have, we believe they must be content.

This reminds me of King Solomon and the book of Ecclesiastes. Solomon had it all—palaces, gold, wives, popularity, and so much more. Compared with today's standards, scholars say he was more than ten times richer than Bill Gates. As he neared the end of his life, he penned this powerful book in the Old Testament, reflecting on everything he had and concluding he still felt unhappy and meaningless. Even though that was thousands of years ago and the stuff may be different today, the reality hasn't changed. We still long for the stuff, don't we? We still haven't learned. Whether or not you're into hip-hop culture, all of us need to be careful, because we live in a society that constantly tries to get us to buy into this mentality.

THE NEW SPIRITUALITY IN HIP-HOP

After Tupac and Biggie were shot, it became cool to talk about God and the afterlife in your music. As an artist who talks about God quite often in his lyrics, I saw a definite shift in people's mindset. In the early 1990s, I launched a hip-hop ministry at my college, and as we rapped at several nonchurch events, we noticed some resistance. When we would roll up to the juvenile detention center or a street concert, people would come up to us and ask us if we were with the church group and if we were going to do church rap. I'd tell them that hip-hop is about expressing what you've been through, and since being changed by God was a part of my experiences, I was going to share about that. Even with that explanation, many of them would roll their eyes, suck their teeth, or make a negative comment.

By the late nineties, all that had changed. During the summer of 2000, I had the opportunity to do seven concerts during a weekend at Rikers Island Prison in New York City, one of the most notorious prisons in the world. At the time, I was traveling with Chuck Colson's Prison Fellowship ministry. They had gone to Rikers every year, and several of the other ministers were telling me stories of people getting stabbed in front of them and fights breaking out. I had been in several prisons before, but I never saw anything too crazy, so I knew this would be interesting. The first day, we ministered in one of the gymnasiums to about three hundred young-adult male inmates. The comedian who went up before me actually got booed off the stage. At that point I was getting a little nervous and really asking God for some favor with these cats. My DJ threw a beat on and I came out and just started sharing what I was about. Suddenly the crowd hushed, instantly respectful, and listened intently. When we got into the music, I had them represent what borough they were from, and they really got into it as they proudly shouted for Brooklyn, the Bronx, Queens, and Manhattan. At the end of the concerts, there were always several guys who would come up to me and thank me for coming and share that they also had written some Christian rap songs. This wasn't some rare event. Ever since the late nineties, this frequently happens everywhere I go. People give me respect for doing Christ-centered rap, and they express that they have written a gospel song or two themselves.

The spirituality aspect popped up more and more as each year passed. DMX put a prayer at the end of each of his albums. In his song "The Prayer V," from his 2003 album, *Grand Champ*, he says, "Father, thank you for making me righteous and accepting me through the blood of Jesus. Because of that I am blessed and highly favored by you." These were truly heartfelt prayers, but the rest of his albums were filled with profanity and violence. When I ministered at a church in another state, the youth pastor excitedly asked me if I had ever heard of a Christian rapper named DMX. He told me that one of the kids in his youth

> They fell for the material entice
> ■ but it's suffice ■ to think
> more twice ■ cuz our shorties'
> and our communities' future
> ain't nice

group had played this prayer rap for him that really impressed him. He had played it in one of his recent services. I asked him if he heard the rest of the album, and he told me no. I filled him in that the rest of the album was full of profanity and content that definitely wouldn't be considered Christ-like. He was shocked and a little embarrassed. This is a prime example of why we must be students of culture and be aware of what's going on in the world of the people we minister to.

In 2002, New York rapper Nas came out with the album *God's Son*. In the song "Heaven," he boldly says,

> If heaven was a mile away and you could ride by the gates,
> would you try to run inside when it opens, would you try to die
>   today?
> Would you pray louder, finally believing his power?
> Even if you couldn't see, but you could feel, would you still doubt
>   him?
> Would you change the way you acting?

In 2002, KRS-One released the album *Spiritual Minded*. Back in the day, KRS was one of my favorite MCs because he usually had something profound to say. He was considered very intelligent and socially conscious.

I was curious but at the same time cautious. Message boards and chat rooms on the internet buzzed with the news of his gospel album. Rumors were flying that he was now a Christian, while others said he wasn't. Around 2002, gospel music was at an all-time high in sales. While most other genres struggled or only grew a little bit, gospel had seen huge increases several years in a row. The industry noticed and artists were noticing. Even though KRS had always been a spiritual guy, he decided to do a Christian album to reach a new audience. But he wasn't a Christian himself, which shows that it can be dangerous for the Christian community to embrace a celebrity too quickly and support them as a minister before they check out the facts. Unfortunately, we don't make sure that the person has been discipled, that they are solid, or in this case, that they are even a true believer. If they have a name, let's sell it! This was the case with KRS. Even after the album dropped, some people defended it, despite several songs that contradicted Christianity.

In 2004, the music scene exploded with spiritual themes. Rock bands like Linkin Park, Evanescence, and Hoobastank each had some challenging soul-searching songs. But the genre of music that blew it up the loudest was hip-hop. LL Cool J and Pharrell, of the Neptunes, both talked about starting gospel labels. DMX claimed

Our music has power but what's its purpose? ▪ just to get rich and die is so worthless

he was going to put his mic down to preach the gospel. R. Kelly put out an inspirational album with the hit single "U Saved Me." Minister Durrell Betha—a hip-hop-artist-turned-pastor known as Mase—even contradicted himself and picked up the mic and released another album. But the biggest splash was the hit song and video of the summer by Kanye West, "Jesus Walks," in which he says,

> So, here goes my single dog, radio needs this.
> They say I can rap about anything except for Jesus.
> That means guns, sex, lies, videotapes,
> but if I talk about God, my record won't get played, huh?

Well, it did get played ... a lot!
Many artists give thanks to Jesus Christ and have some songs with spiritual content. But other songs on their albums are filled with profanity and the degradation of women, stuff that's the opposite of honoring Jesus Christ. It's easy to see the artists' lifestyle choices reflected in their inter-

views and videos, and in the news when they end up in trouble. Working every day with urban youth and adults, I've seen this unfortunate reality really confuse people. Some adopt the attitude that they can be a Christian and still do whatever they want, just like their favorite artist.

CHRIST-CENTERED HIP-HOP

Even before it became popular to mention Jesus in your rhymes, there were several brothers truly putting it down for Christ. These Christian artists used music as a way to connect the culture with the message. Some have called this genre Christian hip-hop or Christian rap, gospel hip-hop or gospel rap, or holy hip-hop. My mom bought me my first Christ-centered hip-hop cassette tape, by a group called JC and the Boyz, back in 1989. It was all right, but it didn't compare to the quality and style that I was used to. She also bought me a tape called *Bible Break* by a rapper named Stephen Wiley. It was geared more toward kids, and to a fourteen-year-old engulfed in the culture, it was corny! I gave up on Christian hip-hop and kept my ear to the streets.

In the early nineties, groups like DC Talk made a big name in the Christian scene. They reached a lot of Christian teens and gave them an alternative, but to a city kid like me, it just sounded like a popcorn imitation. Even after I made a stronger commitment to Christ and went to Bible college, I still listened to secular hip-hop. I'd try to filter it and only listen to the radio, but a lot of it was still pretty negative. In spring 1992, a classmate gave me a tape of a group called the Dynamic Twins. I connected with this album, titled *No Room 2 Breathe*. I was excited to finally find a group that sounded good. Around that time, I was starting to write lyrics again, which was a huge encouragement to me. That summer another friend gave me an SFC album called *Phase Three*. Soon I went to the Christian bookstore to buy up everything I could find in the tiny rap section. E.T.W., P.I.D., Michael Peace, and several others joined my growing tape collection. There was some decent stuff, but a few times I was disappointed with my purchases because the groups were not up to date and sounded plain cheesy.

On some of my trips to Philly, my best friend, Tony Bruno, introduced me to a rapper he met in high school. His name was Brady Goodwin, aka the Phanatik. Goodwin was working with some other rappers who soon started this group called the Cross Movement. I remember getting some underground tapes that they recorded in their basement studios. There was nothing like this in the Christian bookstores. It had a raw, gritty East Coast sound with solid lyrics representing Christ. They had plans to do a professional studio album and hoped to get distribution for it.

During the nineties, several more groups emerged, and the labels put more money behind them, so the quality was slowly improving. A Hispanic artist from California named T-Bone released several albums and built a fan base as he traveled around the country. Gotee Records, formed by Toby Mac and two other partners, became one of the premier urban labels, as Grits, Knowdaverbs, and Out of Eden broke into the contemporary Christian music market. Since then, Gotee has signed several other acts, like DJ Maj, John Reuben, Mars III, and LA Symphony. KJ-52 has become a standout artist, really connecting with the contemporary Christian music market, and has been on

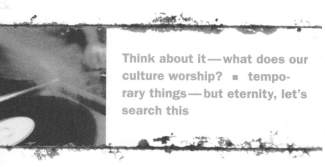

Think about it—what does our culture worship? ■ temporary things—but eternity, let's search this

several large tours with Acquire the Fire, Carmen, and Revolve. The Cross Movement released their first album in 1997 through a small distributor, and then got picked up by Seventh Street Records, which released several albums the next few years. They quickly became the bestselling group on an indie label. By 2004, they signed a major distribution deal with Provident/BMG and released several quality albums with their group and several other solo artists.

Christ-centered hip-hop continues to grow and touch many lives, but at the same time, it is plagued with many obstacles. I've attended summits and planning meetings with industry insiders for years, and we still deal with many of the same problems. Although hip-hop has dominated the mainstream market for many years, it is on the back burner in the Christian market. There is sparse radio support, no full video channels, and no real store support to get the music before the masses. The situation is slowly improving, but we've learned that it takes time. We're still laying the foundation while being patient and diligent. Many of the gatekeepers in the Christian community have resisted hip-hop because it's so foreign to them. But things are changing as Christian music sales have fallen in 2004 and 2005 and the influence of hip-hop reaches into these gatekeepers' homes through their own kids. They now see that this culture needs to be engaged with the message of Christ.

At the same time, there are some traditionally minded people who aren't open to new forms of ministry. There is a small movement in predominantly African-American Pentecostal circles that actually preaches that hip-hop is not redeemable and that there is no way God can use it. They contend that believers shouldn't engage this culture because it is hopeless. However, this view is simply unbiblical, since Christ came to redeem all cultures and people groups.

On a more positive note, many artists are being distributed in the mainstream, where most Christian artists desire to be. But the reality still remains that the support of the Christian community will be the thing that will get the mainstream to notice. I believe God is maturing the leaders and artists of this emerging movement. When it's his time, he'll open doors. But in the meantime, artists must be faithful in the mission fields he has given them.

THE FUTURE OF HIP-HOP

Industry leaders have proclaimed that the years 2000 to 2005 have proven to be the biggest years yet for hip-hop music. During the week I was writing this in 2006, according to *Billboard*, the top five music videos on MTV and BET were all hip-hop/R&B, four out of five of the top five albums were hip-hop/R&B, and all five radio singles fell into that category. It's not hard to see that this music and its cultural influence dominate popular culture. Hip-hop's current level of popularity won't always be the same. That would be impossible. But it's safe to say that the hip-hop culture is not going away. It is going to have major influence for years to come, evolving and changing as it shapes society and as society shapes it.

> Dig deep you'll find a creator's love that's so perfect ■ manifested in Christ—he worked it—offers forgiveness and hope, that's why I proudly spit him in verses "

It has become easy to predict what the content of the next number-one secular hip-hop hit will be. Even though the music is on top right now, a growing number of people are expressing how repetitive and bland the culture has become. An underground movement of people who want something different is growing. They desire something intelligent, productive, and real. Many people in the culture in their twenties and thirties (both Christian and not Christian) I've spoken with can't stand what's being played on the radio. "Keep it real" has been hip-hop's motto for years, yet it's rarely practiced. The culture, though still searching for something real, has been plagued with contradictions and confusion. Looking at Scripture, I see that not everyone will build a relationship with Christ. But I do hope that, with God's help, we can make more of an impact and help shape the future of hip-hop as we lead people to truth.

PART THREE

church ■ hip-hop ■ culture

An Unorthodox Approach

Ministry to the Culture

8

Redefining Urban

Hip-hop is often referred to as urban music because of its origin in the urban center of New York City. But what does the word urban really mean? Today urban is less a location and more of a mindset, which in turn has a direct impact on how we connect with the urban community. Let me explain.

I recently participated in an urban leaders' summit in which we talked about a subject that has been at the forefront for urban ministry leaders the past few years. Urban centers are rapidly changing, and the landscape looks a lot different in many cities. Society recognizes this new reality, but it seems that the church is again a step behind what's really going on. In the past, the term urban generally referred to inner-city areas where poverty, crime, and the concentration of minorities were high. Because of redevelopment and gentrification, this has changed in many cities. During the 1960s and 1970s, as city neighborhoods aged, masses of middle-class people exited to the suburbs, lured by new housing and more space, a phenomenon referred to as "the great white flight." These aging neighborhoods were taken over by lower-income residents, many of whom were minorities. Unfortunately, as the middle-class residents left, so did many of the churches, following their members to the suburbs. Churches do exist in most city neighborhoods, but it is hard to find one with adequate resources and the ability to make a significant impact in its community.

Over time, the first ring of suburbs filled up and people moved farther from the city's core, igniting urban sprawl. Yet suburbanites still worked in the downtown districts, making commutes longer. But thanks to rising fuel costs, increased time pressures, and the disconnectedness of bedroom communities, people looked for a way to return to urban areas.

Many urban areas have now become hip, yuppie, and expensive with "exposed wall" condos and high-rise lofts taking over what was once the inner city. In turn, the hood has now moved out and taken root in the first ring of suburbs, outside the city limits. I've seen this transition happen over the past decade in Tampa. What had been the ghetto for years has become an entertainment district just outside of downtown called Ybor City. It's an old neighborhood with a lot of history, but as nightclubs and bars moved in along the main street in the early nineties, it transitioned from the place you avoided to a popular weekend hangout. By the late nineties, the area had become so cool that people bought empty run-down buildings and converted them to residential lofts, chic retail stores, and trendy clubs. Rents and condo prices are now higher than in the suburbs. It's the "in" place to live, within walking distance from entertainment and just a few minutes from downtown.

American Dream

66 The first immigrants came in search of religious freedom ▪ they found wealth and said forget God, we don't need him ▪ we can beat him ▪ never let their little kids meet him

Unfortunately, this comes at a cost. The Housing and Urban Development Authority (HUD) is tearing down housing projects or having private companies run them, driving out the low-income tenants in favor of working-class residents. The idea is to create a diverse socioeconomic and cultural blend, but the result many times is to push the poor out of the city. Some of the worst neighborhoods in the Tampa area are now just outside the city limits, while the areas where the poor used to live are filled with working-class residents and even some upper-class people. Statistically, we don't have fewer low-income people; they're just more spread out. So you end up back at square one: high concentrations of lower-income people living together, inevitably creating a downward-spiraling environment where poverty flourishes and hope and ambition are lost. I've seen this firsthand in the "projects" near our church. This small neighborhood filled with drug dealers, pregnant teens, fatherless households, and little discipline is the only world these people know.

So where am I going with this? To illustrate the point that urban is now more of a mindset than a location. Not only is the urban locale changing, but hip-hop, MTV, and the internet have pipelined this lifestyle to the suburbs and beyond.

INFECTING THE SUBURBS

Even though hip-hop has its roots in the rough inner city, it has become the identity of many suburbanites of emerging generations. The urban mindset has spread well beyond the city limits. In fact, hip-hop achieved its dominance because of the economic force of suburban dollars.

According to *Forbes*, "Hip-hop is no longer the music or culture of a particular ethnic group. Hip-hop has grown well beyond the urban market since the genre's first hit, 'Rapper's Delight,' was released in 1979.... Its customer base is the 45 million hip-hop consumers between the ages of 13–34, 80 percent of whom are white."[16] According to Simmons Media Group research, this same group has one trillion dollars in spending power.

These facts show that the culture in which we live has changed. Things were much different ten or fifteen years ago. Unfortunately, the church, by and large, hasn't acknowledged this shift. Youth ministry hasn't grasped it. Many large ministry organizations haven't come to grips with it either. Publishers and ministry-resource companies busily produce material from a pre-urban mindset—material that doesn't engage its audience like it could or should. The church, for the most part, still believes that anything urban-oriented is only for the inner-city or ethnic crowd. This couldn't be farther from the truth.

Since the midnineties, I've had the opportunity to travel to numerous churches and ministry events to perform (rap), speak, and share my story. Well over half of these hundred events are at suburban churches. And I'm not the only one who's experiencing this. Other national Christian hip-hop artists say the same thing. Don't get me wrong. It's great that many suburban ministries are using hip-hop as a tool to reach teens for Christ, but it can't just be an occasional concert to engage them. We have to create relevant models for weekly worship services and discipleship. I've had several suburban youth pastors tell me that most of their teens disengage during worship and with their youth ministry as a whole. Many of these pastors don't understand it and are wondering what they're doing wrong.

AN UNORTHODOX APPROACH: MINISTRY TO THE CULTURE

These are guys who have been to the big conferences and invested in all kinds of resources and programs. I'm not bashing any conferences or curriculums, but many of the people putting these things together still haven't realized the depth of the shift that has taken place. They still train youth ministers to do youth ministry with a pre-urban style.

Many youth pastors and senior pastors grew up listening to rock or contemporary styles of music, and this personal preference is reflected in their worship services. I've seen this in settings where all but a handful of the entire youth group or young-adult group were into urban music. When challenged to blend the style or switch it up to be more relevant to the crowd, the pastors quickly comment that it's not about style; it's about worshiping God. But for some of these leaders, it *is* about style, because many people are being held back from engaging in worship like they could. Stylistically, worship shouldn't be so foreign or separate from our everyday lives. In Romans 12:1, Paul talks about worship being part of everything we do. There must be some cultural connections with worship or younger generations will feel like you're changing them into your cookie-cutter image.

Send 'em to college, it's all about succeeding ■ get rich or die trying as the greed keeps feeding

Of course, not every kid in the suburbs is solely into hip-hop and the urban mindset, but these are major influences that we can't ignore. In 1999, I performed at a suburban church in Florida for a youth group of about 150 teens. Only about ten of them were really into hip-hop, so it was a tough crowd. A little over two years later, they asked me to come back again, and I honestly wondered why. But when the music started and I stepped onto the stage, it was a totally different environment. Not only had the group grown in size, but they were on their feet, moving to the music. As I looked into the crowd, I saw that the scenario had flipped. In this group of close to three hundred, only 10 percent was not into hip-hop. I wondered whether I was at the same place. It was an incredible night of ministry, as several teens built new relationships with Christ. I even recognized several teens who had been the wallflowers before but had changed their style and were in their comfort zone now.

This shift happened fast and is happening fast in many communities. Many suburban youth groups consist predominantly of hip-hop enthusiasts, yet their leaders are still worshiping with a rock band. "Why aren't

112

they into it?" they wonder. Just ask the kids what music they listen to on their iPods. If they're honest, they're like the majority of American teens and young adults who are inspired by and connected to hip-hop. Style, approach, and atmosphere are key to people in emerging generations, and they demand relevance. This goes for urban and suburban churches alike.

For instance, although Crossover is located in the city limits of Tampa, we have become a regional church. Several people travel thirty minutes to an hour to be a part of our worship and community because we're the only church reaching this culture and generation in this way. Take Carl and Ann Zalak, a married couple in their late twenties. They have traveled an hour and a half one way (three hours round-trip) to our church every weekend for over four years to serve and be involved. Carl is a successful small-business owner with several employees, and Ann is a stay-at-home mom. They're not youth or college kids anymore, but they grew up on hip-hop. Today, they connect on a spiritual level with the hip-hop scene at Crossover.

> But they can take their words and eat 'em ∎ when this world leaves 'em bleeding ∎ I'll pull their card meaning ∎ this ain't Hallmark or American Greeting

Five years ago, Shelby Stelhin came with a friend to our Thursday night youth service so he could practice his budding break-dance moves afterward. Shelby was a fifteen-year-old white kid from a suburban area in Tampa, nearly forty minutes away. He thought he was going to a club in Tampa. When he arrived, he hesitated to come inside because he had little church experience. He didn't come for church; he came to dance! Intrigued, he watched people who looked just like him passionately enter into worship with music that even he was feeling. Although he came in acting hard and with a skeptical attitude, by the end of the night, he had tears in his eyes as he built a new relationship with Christ. Despite coming from a home that wasn't Christian and living a good distance away, he made his way to Crossover throughout his high-school years. It's been exciting to watch him grow, get discipled, and develop a true hunger for Scripture and truth. Today, Shelby is an active member at Crossover. He leads a small group Bible study for break dancers and hosts several break-dancing events at the church throughout the year. Shelby has traveled internationally with the Fla.vor Alliance to minister with his story and his dance skills. He's transferred his passion into a job as a performer at amusement parks like Busch Gardens and Sea World.

MULTICULTURALISM

It didn't matter that Shelby was from the suburbs or that he was a white male in a multicultural crowd in which he was actually in the minority. That type of atmosphere is exactly what emerging generations want. Our church is multicultural not only because it reflects the surrounding community but also because it reflects the worldview of younger generations. Unlike previous generations, they *want* to mix it up. Among younger generations, relationships and marriages of people from different ethnic backgrounds and races have been on the rise. I noticed this growing up in Philadelphia. I had friends of all different backgrounds. I dated girls of different races and generally gave it little thought. My peers didn't see this as out of the ordinary or progressive. But the older generation, including my parents, didn't always approve. The result: my wife, Lucy, is Puerto Rican, and I'm mixed, though predominantly Greek. When most people see us together, they assume I'm also Hispanic. But even though my appearance might put

James 5—ya'll better do some reading ▪ and turn your lights on ▪ your finances will be gone ▪ like WorldCom and Enron

me in that category, our backgrounds were much different. My family had some ethnic flavor, but we certainly didn't speak Spanish at home or cook authentic Puerto Rican food like Lucy's family did. While this was all new to me, it also made her even more exciting and attractive. Likewise, there were many things about my background that were new and different to my wife. Although previous generations might have looked at these things as barriers, to us it wasn't a big deal. People our age weren't telling us to think twice about our relationship. We have an incredible relationship and our families genuinely love each other.

This is a key point for ministry to the younger generation. Teens and young adults today are getting more and more outside of the traditional race box. They are mixed not only ethnically but also racially. Predictably, this is most common in metropolitan areas. But like urban music and culture, it extends beyond the traditional city lines to the broader suburban community. *USA Today* said it well in an article about this phenomenon: "Race lines clearly blur in areas such as music or clothing as young people of different races adopt styles rooted in other cultures. Rap music may have mostly black roots, but it has become such an important musical genre that rappers are now of all races."[17]

Don Coleman, CEO of GlobalHue, a multicultural advertising agency, reiterated the point: "The new broad base is multi-cultural in my opinion. That's really the new generational market. In their minds 'urban' in advertising is more edgy and has a certain attitude that is 'mainstream.' It's acceptable now if you run an ad targeted for an African-American market in the general market."[18]

Finally, David Harris, a sociology professor at Cornell University, takes a long-term view of this surge in multiracial identification: "Over time, they [the younger generation] may simplify their race and be treated as members of a single racial group. Just because you're multiracial as a five-year-old does not necessarily mean you'll be multiracial as a 50 year old."[19]

Again and again, I hear people express how excited they are to see and be a part of the diversity at our church. This is the church of the future. We are moving into a post-white, post-Hispanic, post-black, post-Asian church! We must recognize this and adapt our approach.

SUBGENRES OF HIP-HOP

Not all hip-hop music is alike, nor are all aspects of the culture alike. The culture has been around for over thirty years, and several different styles and subcultures have evolved. There's not a one-size-fits-all worldview in hip-hop, so there's not a one-size-fits-all approach to engaging the culture and communicating Christ. Let's start with the music.

There are five main subgenres of hip-hop music: East Coast, West Coast, Dirty South, Midwest, and Reggaeton. East Coast originated in New York and has the distinct flavor of hip-hop produced from the northeastern cities. It is known to be more lyrical, intellectual, and gritty with the beats. West Coast originated in California in the late eighties and eventually dominated the scene in the early nineties, since it was the place gangsta rap was born. What makes West Coast stand out is the accent and the content. The Dirty South style emerged in the late nineties and is still a hot commodity. The beats per minute are faster, the rappers have that Southern twang, and the lyrics are generally simple. The songs usually have catchy hooks and danceable beats, which made this style especially popular in clubs. As each geographical area tried to get on the map, the Midwest style eventually emerged as a mixture of the other three styles, but with distinctions in the style, flow, and accent that made it stand out a little differently.

Reggaeton is the newest genre to emerge in the U.S. With roots in Puerto Rico and the Caribbean, it's now becoming a big thing here in the States, especially on commercial radio. This style has a repetitive double-time rhythm, and most lyrics are rapped and sung in Spanish. Despite the language barrier, several of the songs have made their way into regular rotation on hip-hop stations throughout the U.S. Recently, several Reggaeton artists even started collaborating with English-speaking hip-hop artists. This subgenre has been the bestselling music in Puerto Rico and several other islands the past few years and is gaining market share in the U.S.

Although each of these styles is different, they have many things in common. Several artists from one geographical area have done songs or even adapted styles from other parts of the country. Several rappers from the Northeast have done Dirty South–style songs, and you can also listen to some West Coast rappers and think they are straight from New York. So a lot of intermeshing takes place. With these different subgenres come differences in slang, dress, and sometimes even values.

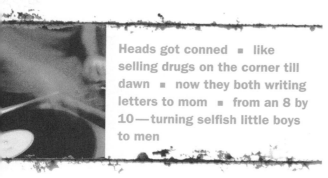

Heads got conned ■ like selling drugs on the corner till dawn ■ now they both writing letters to mom ■ from an 8 by 10—turning selfish little boys to men

There are also different content subgenres, and new ones seem to be popping up all the time. The two main content subgenres are underground and mainstream or commercial. Commercial or mainstream is usually more radio friendly with catchy hooks and concepts that aren't as deep. Most commercial hip-hop is repetitive and talks about materialism, sex, or with unabashed arrogance, the artists themselves.

Underground hip-hop can be classified as hip-hop that hasn't made it into the mainstream yet, but many times it won't ever make the mainstream because of its style and content. Underground hip-hop generally has more substantive content and intellect, and interestingly, it's typically more positive. Some artists will actually begin to water down or alter their content so they can cross over to the mainstream, though this is often looked down upon by their fans and classified as selling out. Underground hip-hop has an endless number of subgenres, including conscious hip-hop, spiritual hip-hop, political hip-hop, and Christian hip-hop. Because hip-hop is growing in other countries, there are also country-specific genres that take on the characteristics of that culture and language.

There's not a one-size-fits-all approach to reaching this audience. What works in New York won't work the same way in Los Angeles, and what works in Tampa won't work the same way in Mississippi. You must research your community and your young people to see what style of hip-hop they are into. Most of our congregation and a large part of our community are from the Northeast, so we cater to the East Coast style. We mix in some Reggaeton because of our large Hispanic population, and we mix in some Dirty South because of its rise in popularity and relevance. We try to be diverse, but we also know where our community is and what our strengths are.

GLOBAL IMPACT

The urban mindset hasn't infected just the U.S. It has become global. And so too has the challenge facing the church. While Europe and the Far East adopted hip-hop at an alarming pace, the relevance of the church remains stagnant. And so the hip-hop culture is a whole new mission field that must be reached.

I've had the opportunity to travel to Germany, the UK, and Japan over the past few years. I was astonished to find German teens and young adults in a small village wearing all the latest hip-hop clothing brands and listening to the latest American hip-hop artists. As we drove through the countryside, I was amazed to see a farm silo tagged with a big graffiti mural! How did the influence of American urban culture reach all the way to rural Germany? The answer is they had MTV, and that's all they watched. They lived on the internet and subscribed to hip-hop magazines. It was what they identified with.

A ministry based in Germany brought four of us from Crossover to speak and do concerts in public schools and in their version of a community youth center for five days. We had two rappers, a DJ, and a break-dancer with us. The German teens were ecstatic to be able to meet and hang out with American hip-hop artists. This gave us an incredible platform to represent Christ and share how he has impacted our lives as hip-hoppers. They were astonished that we were actually cool and authentic and that we really loved God. They never saw this in their native country, since most churches were very traditional. Even the progressive leaders were barely aware of the subculture of hip-hop, still in its first generation in Western Europe.

Our host, Ralph, shared his frustrations. His sentiments—though expressed in broken English and nuanced with German culture—sounded just like the feedback I hear every day in the States. Many teens hung out at the youth center, but few would ever respond to spiritual things and get committed. Ralph had been there a few years, and although God greatly used him, only a handful of teens had committed to following Christ. He was struggling to connect.

While hip-hop was the bridge, there was a much greater chasm to cross in the small village in the German countryside. They had a large Turkish population that was primarily Muslim, and several of the Turkish teens came to the youth center every time the doors were open. In addition, the liberal German culture was a major impediment. Prostitution is legal, porn is on regular TV, there is no age restriction for smoking, and you can drink alcohol at age sixteen. To top it off, this seemingly unchurched place was in fact dominated by "members" of the church. Yet their version of church was to pay a small tax mandated by the government for church members as a form of penance. Attend church once a year, pay your tax, live however you want.

While it was a tough place to do mission work, we broke through in our short time there. Surprising to us, most of the teens could speak some English, and some were fluent. We did several concerts, we preached, and because of their persistent begging, we even did some hip-hop-style worship with our DJ. That was the first time, and the only time to date, that I led worship with my crew of nonsingers. But God used it to inspire a true time of worship, and many teens for the first time joined in singing to their creator. Over the

Now suddenly God's their friend ▪ it's humbling like the Prodigal Son in the pig pen ▪ you can't trust Big Ben ▪ green paper will burn ▪ wake up and see that Elohim makes the world turn

years, I've done several large events with thousands of people, but that time with 150 people packed into the little youth center in the Westerwald countryside of Germany was a special moment that will forever be etched in my mind. That week, forty-eight people at the youth center responded to build a new relationship with Christ—Turkish Muslims and Germans alike! It was a true outpouring of God's Spirit in such a hardened place. We returned the following year to have another incredible week of ministry with Ralph and his team. Although this was a cross-cultural missions trip, we had so much in common with the teens there culturally. Hip-hop was the bridge.

I had a similar experience in Japan a few years ago when the United States Air Force brought me and seven other members of Fla.vor Alliance, the group of hip-hop artists from Crossover, to Yokota Air Force Base in Tokyo. We were the entertainment for their big Fourth of July bash on the base. They knew we were Christians and that we did positive Christ-centered hip-hop. I can't explain why they chose us to come instead of the Baha Men, creators of the one-hit wonder "Who Let the Dogs Out?" Because it was a government-funded event, we had to sign a contract agreeing that we wouldn't preach at the main show. Normally we present the gospel in our concerts and in sharing our story, so this was definitely a roadblock. However, we prayerfully agreed to abide by their house rules and committed to let the Lord work.

We rocked a crowd of more than three thousand at the event and simply let our lyrics speak for themselves. We were also allowed to sell our CDs and DVDs and to perform at several events off the base. Of course, God showed up and did his thing. Dozens of men and women committed their lives to Christ, and although we came for the Americans, we saw many Japanese in attendance feel the Holy Spirit.

Like many other American influences, hip-hop has become huge in Japan. Japanese youth and young adults are going to tanning beds to get darker and are dreading and braiding their hair. Many of them seem really disconnected from their Japanese roots and embrace American hip-hop as their new identity. They have walked away from Eastern traditions and, more pointedly, their parents' Eastern religions, opening the door for searching and discovery—and for Christianity. This type of thing is happening in countries across the globe as hip-hop culture has become a global voice of emerging generations.

To bring this East-meets-West connection full circle, in November 2005 we featured Elijah, a Japanese rapper, at our annual Fla.vor Fest conference. I met him through a pastor in California who mentors me. This unique rapper has his own Christ-centered hip-hop CD, which is totally in Japanese. It's really cool to listen to, and it was fun to watch the crowd go crazy when he performed at the fest's evening concert. Elijah was truly a servant, arriving early and offering to help our team set up for the conference. He has a real heart for Japanese youth and is working on planting a church in Japan that will target youth and young adults

> The American Dream ▪ it's not all that it seems ▪ from the ghetto to Wall Street, it's money-making schemes

who are into hip-hop. Even while he was in Tampa for Fla.vor Fest, he ministered to a Japanese exchange student who came to the concert. He spent an entire day with him after the event and ministered to him. Since then Elijah has joined our church family to intern with us for a year so he can be trained to plant his ministry. He is also building relationships with Japanese students who are studying at the University of South Florida, fifteen minutes from our church campus.

Elijah represents this new emerging thought process. People of all ages are realizing that hip-hop culture is a whole new mission field that must be reached. But just because they live down the street doesn't mean that we speak the same language and value the same things. Elijah and thousands of others just like him seek out training to be missionaries to the hip-hop culture. Whether or not they are indigenous to the culture, these hip-hop evangelists still need leadership training, biblically and culturally. The church as a whole must begin to provide classroom teaching, internships, and resources to equip people with these callings.

HIP-HOP HAS GROWN UP

As I travel across the country doing workshops, speaking engagements, and concerts, I often hear the same comment: "That's a great thing you guys are doing for those kids," or "That's a great thing you guys are doing for the youth." Now, God definitely uses us to reach a lot of kids and youth. It's been amazing to watch God touch their lives, from young children with issues to thugged-out teens in high school. But to be honest, these comments about it being just for kids and youth are somewhat frustrating to me. Why? Because, quite frankly, many people just don't get it. Our church actually reaches more adults than kids and teens com-

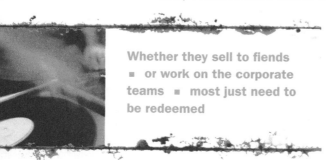

Whether they sell to fiends ▪ or work on the corporate teams ▪ most just need to be redeemed

bined. I'm not saying one group is more important than the other. I was the youth pastor full time for six years, and then still led the high-school ministry for another four years while I was the senior pastor. These kids need God as much as anyone, but so do the adults at our church. While our congregation skews younger and is predominantly in their twenties, thirties, and forties, they aren't kids, and they aren't youth. They're adults who are still into hip-hop culture. They have jobs, families, and college degrees. In fact, many marketing firms all around the world seem to understand this, and they push their products especially to this emerging demographic of twenty- and thirtysomethings. But the church is missing the boat.

When a megacorporation like Chrysler uses Snoop Dogg in their commercials with Lee Iacocca, you can see how broad hip-hop's influence has become. Hertz had a commercial featuring a DMX song with retired couples getting out of sports cars and Hummers and strutting to the beat. This is marketing genius. People from every generation can watch a commercial like that and find it humorous, and it makes a lasting impression.

Hip-hop is crossing generational lines. Jeep has worked with Missy Elliott, while Snoop and 50 Cent have helped propel the image of vehicles such as the Chrysler 300 and the Cadillac Escalade. If you open your eyes, you'll quickly see hip-hop being used to sell all kinds of products. Church leaders need to take serious note of these things.

Urban style and culture magazine *Vibe* claimed a few years ago that a quarter of their readers were actually over thirty-five years old. With more than 1.8 million readers, it is considered the largest urban-lifestyle, hip-

The American Dream ■ it's not all that it seems ■ from the ghetto to Wall Street, it's money-making schemes

hop-flavored magazine. How could a quarter of their readers be over thirty-five? Simple math. This culture developed in the South Bronx in the 1970s and quickly dominated urban landscapes in the 1980s. In the 1990s, it broke through into the mainstream. And today hip-hop defines mainstream pop culture; now the percentage of people in their twenties who are into hip-hop is even higher than it used to be.

These are important facts to think about, especially when these age groups (particularly twenties and thirties) are becoming almost nonexistent in many churches. Barna.org states that "a majority of twentysomethings—61% of today's young adults—had been churched at one point during their teen years but they are now spiritually disengaged (i.e., not actively attending church, reading the Bible, or praying). Only one-fifth of twentysomethings (20%) have maintained a level of spiritual activity consistent with their high school experiences."[20] When it comes to using hip-hop as a tool to reach people, church leaders usually assume it's just for the youth group. Yes, many teens enjoy it, and it's an effective tool to reach them. But we should realize that when people turn eighteen, their musical and cultural tastes don't suddenly change. That's the part many still don't get.

BUILDING BRIDGES

The topic of reaching the hip-hop culture is a passion of mine, and I've been afforded the chance to share my experiences and viewpoint at several conferences and events. First I make my case, and then often I open up the floor and ask people their opinion on why churches assume using hip-hop is just for the youth group. I get a lot of great responses and want to share a few.

Jose from California shared, "Older people don't understand the culture, and they are scared of it." Christy from Oregon said, "Some in my church think hip-hop can be used in the youth room, but it's not holy enough for the main sanctuary." Ron from the Bronx added, "The older generations have been poisoned by the media to get only a negative perspective about hip-hop." Mary from Wisconsin: "Church leaders don't prefer that type of music and they are not willing to change anything." Mike from Florida: "The church is generally way behind what's going on around them in society, and many of the older people don't even realize how big hip-hop has become."

So what's the solution to some of these issues? It's not a simple formula. Humans resist change. We all have our preferences, routines, and habits. That's how we're wired. Some of Christ's last words and instructions are found in Matthew 28 and Acts 1. When someone is preparing to leave for a long time or is on their deathbed, their last words are the most critical. What were Jesus' last words? Go into the world to reach people

From suits and ties to Tims and jeans ▪ most just need to be redeemed "

and disciple them. If we are truly passionate about that, then we have to be willing to change somewhat. It's all about building bridges between generations.

Believers of different generations may have many different tastes and backgrounds, but there are still many things we all have in common. Fulfilling the Great Commission should be a centerpiece. How can we work together to fulfill our corporate mandate? It takes a lot of education and comfort-zone crashing. Ron from the Bronx may have hit on one of the biggest obstacles. Many in the older generations, especially in light of the media's influence, have a very negative mindset about the urban and hip-hop culture. I honestly don't blame people for this mindset. I always try to put myself in other people's shoes, and if the only thing I knew about hip-hop was what I heard on the news or what I heard at the stoplight when I pulled up next to a young person's car, then I would probably be pretty skeptical about how God could use it. Emerging leaders and established leaders need to see the desperate need at hand. We must dialog and pray together as we seek new cultural models for what the New Testament church needs to look like in today's culture.

People assume that if you target hip-hop culture, you'll exclude the majority or you'll just be boxing yourself in and serving a small group of

people. It's really the opposite. In most metropolitan areas, if you don't engage this culture, you're actually excluding the majority of people in these
emerging generations. I challenge you to wrestle with this. I'm not saying
that every ministry needs to do things the way we do. Not at all! We each
have unique God-given visions, callings, and gifts. But I am advocating
that something needs to be done in your church, in your community, and,
if you have teens or young adults, even in your own home.

As the body of Christ, our responsibility, according to the Great Commission, is to reach all people. We must recognize this people group—
those who identify with hip-hop culture—as a huge and diverse mission
field right on our very own doorsteps. Maybe your church can start a hip-
hop outreach ministry. Maybe you'll try a separate service once a month.
Maybe you could support another ministry already doing it, adding your
resources, mentorship, or finances to their passion. Maybe you'll even
blend some new things into your existing worship services.

All of these things require prayer and the right people leading the
charge. It can't be a gimmick to try to attract new people to fill your seats. It
has to be authentic and led by individuals who are being true to themselves
and have developed a passion to reach this people group. The church must
unite and engage this culture, or we will lose the next generation.

9

The Postmodern Hip-Hop Worldview

If you spend time with the younger generation, it's not hard to detect that their worldview is different from previous generations. There has been a major shift in belief systems. Past generations lived in the modern culture, a time when people shared a universal worldview and a common moral view. The modern culture did away with superstition and myths, claiming that most things could be proved or disproved by science. Things were more systematic and logical, truth was absolute, and there was a high emphasis on individualism. Now we are in the throes of postmodernism, although we are still trying to figure out exactly what postmodernism is. It's not easy to pinpoint because it is still developing and the whole culture is fluid. There are many different opinions about what defines postmodernism. Even those who call themselves postmodern describe it in various ways. Some believe postmodernism is beautiful, while others fear it.

ATTEMPTING TO DEFINE POSTMODERNISM

Some say that postmodernism represents a new historical period that we are entering, while others view it as an extension of some of the basic concepts of modernism itself. Still others see postmodernism as an in-between period when old ways are being questioned but the new era has yet to arrive. The Columbia Encyclopedia describes postmodernism as "a term used to designate a multitude of trends—in the arts, philosophy, religion, technology, and many other areas—that come after and deviate from the many twentieth-century movements that constituted modernism. In general, the postmodern view is cool, ironic, and accepting of the fragmentation of contemporary existence. It tends to concentrate on surfaces rather than depths, to blur the distinctions between high and low culture, and as a whole to challenge a wide variety of traditional cultural values."[21]

One thing that most can agree on is that postmodernism is a melting pot of beliefs with no standard worldview. Therefore, people with this pluralistic worldview are highly skeptical of explanations which claim to be valid for everyone regardless of their culture, race, or tradition. They focus on the relative truths of each person. Interpretation is up to the individual. Truth is really whatever you want it to be. Although this current wave of thinking has brought many new obstacles, there

What We Do Now

66 In the year 1973 AD—the time I was born ▪ the Supreme Court passed an issue and this country was torn ▪ the public roared ▪ tempers soared ▪ it could have been me if my mom didn't know the Lord .

have been some positive results, such as a new appreciation for diversity and multiculturalism, the shifting of leadership in younger organizations to more of a team model, and a longing for real community despite trust issues. In the past few years, a big conversation has been going on in the Christian community about postmodernism and the emerging church. It's also become known as the emergent movement. Leaders have tried to figure out how we can communicate truth to a group of people who believe that truth is relative. Several books, conferences, websites, and blogs tackle this complex subject. Yet the majority of people involved in this dialog have been suburban people who are not a part of the emerging urban culture. What does postmodernism look like in an urban/hip-hop context? What differences are there, if any?

Both postmodernism and hip-hop have influenced culture as a whole. There are some distinctions between the two, but overall there are many characteristics that merge, since hip-hop has been influenced by postmodernism. In their book *Hip-Hop and Philosophy*, Derrick Darby and Tommie Shelby write, "Hip-hop not only disrupts many classical disciplines and approaches to knowledge, but challenges theories of modernity by publicly holding them in contempt. So instead of being fixed, hip-hop identities are resolute. Instead of being fluid, they flow."[22] In my experience in an urban setting, I've found that the majority of people in emerging generations are not familiar with the term postmodernism. Although many of its characteristics describe them, they'd be much quicker to say they are part of hip-hop rather than postmodernism.

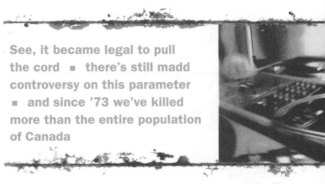

See, it became legal to pull the cord ■ there's still madd controversy on this parameter ■ and since '73 we've killed more than the entire population of Canada

URBAN POSTMODERNISM AND SPIRITUALITY

When I think about the hip-hop worldview, the spiritual aspect jumps out at me the most. I can't remember a time when I had to convince someone from hip-hop culture that God exists. Most of them consider themselves to be spiritual and believe there is a God. Which God or how many gods is where the dilemma comes in. The universal fifth element of hip-hop is known as knowledge or knowledge of self. I've heard some take this to a spiritual level and say they look inside themselves to find God. Many say they are Christians, as do several popular artists, but then they live however they want since they believe there are no absolute boundaries. Some people with ethnic backgrounds connect better culturally with Muslim beliefs, Five Percenters, or the Nation of Islam. These belief systems focus on their racial pride and the oppression they have faced. All three belief systems share allegiances to Allah and the Qur'an but vary on some details and the ethnic emphasis.

The funny thing is that I have rarely met a hip-hopper in these groups who considers themselves a true believer or a fundamentalist. I recently talked with a Muslim I'm building a relationship with who told me that he isn't a fundamentalist Muslim since he has no beard, has piercings and tattoos, and occasionally drinks alcohol. So it's not just Christians in urban emerging generations who technically don't follow all the teachings of their religion. It is an across-the-board feeling that "I'll follow the things that I like, and the rest I'll throw out the window." There's also the dilemma that many people believe in Jesus' teachings along with the teachings of Allah and others. The consensus is that all of these roads lead to God, a prime characteristic of postmodernism.

People with these types of spiritual beliefs typically aren't concerned that you don't share their views. We recently interviewed several people at a local urban flea market for a message series at Crossover that dealt with the historical reliability of the Bible and accounts of Jesus' life. A local

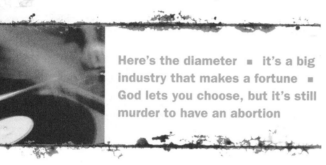

Here's the diameter ■ it's a big industry that makes a fortune ■ God lets you choose, but it's still murder to have an abortion

hip-hop artist was quick to say, "If the Bible brings you closer to God and brings you peace, then go ahead and follow it. I'm personally Muslim, and we as Muslims love Jesus. We believe he was a gift to mankind; we just don't believe he was God's Son. But if you believe he was and that makes you a better person, then that's great." Then we met a hat vendor who allowed us to put some flyers on her countertop. She expressively told us that our church was doing phenomenal things. By her response, we assumed she was a believer or had some church background. But when we interviewed her, we were shocked. She really didn't believe much of the Bible at all. She believed Jesus wasn't God's Son, that he slept around, and that he never was crucified. Yet at the end, she wanted to come to the church and check it out.

Many argue that they have a relationship with God and that he knows their heart. This has become the popular excuse of our culture today, giving us license to bend the Scriptures, change the standards, or give us an exception. Of course God is merciful and full of love. We've all messed up, and none of us deserves to be forgiven. Yet God sacrificed his Son so that we can experience forgiveness and reconnect with our creator. Nevertheless, this gift comes with a commitment to live for him and represent him in all we do. That's the part that many people in the hip-hop culture simply don't get. They buy into the mentality that they can create a relationship with God on their own terms. The media and everyone else around them tell them that's how to do it, so why not? This is definitely rough terrain, but there is hope!

Surreal is a hip-hop artist in Tampa. He is well known in the underground scene because he was the reigning freestyle champion for several years. He was also part of a local group that produced an album and opened up for several major acts when they came through town. Surreal was always a socially conscious person and believed in spirituality, though he believed the Bible was altered from its original form and full of political propaganda. Even though he felt this way, when I listened to his album, I heard him searching for something better. Some of his lyrics had positive morals and mentioned God. A friend of his at work talked to him about Christ and gave him a Jesus movie to check out. That weekend, some of his crew headed out to an event in Orlando, but he decided to stay home and watch the movie. God spoke to him in a big way. He found out the next day that his friends got in a terrible car accident and one of his close friends was killed. It rocked his world. It could have been him. At that moment, he built a relationship with Christ.

Shortly after, he attended our church and grew in his relationship with Christ. He was hungry. It was really exciting to see a brother so far from God now on fire for him in every area of his life. I had the privilege to marry him and his live-in girlfriend. He began bringing all kinds of friends in his circle of influence to our church. He carefully and prayerfully contin-ued rhyming in the secular venues, but he used it as a platform to represent Christ. Surreal and his wife recently had a beautiful baby boy, and he finished up his first Christ-centered hip-hop album. He recently received international distri-bution and has been touring in Europe. Just a few years

First it was in dirty theaters, but the business has risen ▪ to convenience stores, grocery markets, and even your tele-vision ▪ but there's a new division

ago, he was a lost urban postmodern cat who didn't believe, and today he's a hip-hop missionary taking the gospel beyond our city and even over-seas. His story should give us all hope!

QUESTIONS AND MORE QUESTIONS

The modern church doesn't have room for a lot of questions. The mod-ern church simply announces an idea, shares some proof, and expects everyone to accept it. This used to work when we were in a predominantly modern culture, but it doesn't work well for emerging postmodern genera-tions. The modern era declared that there was no place for questioning anything spiritual. We had no right to question. But if we look at Scripture, we can see people wrestling, crying, and shouting out their questions to God. When ministering to this type of crowd, you have to set aside time before and after for questions and answers. I'll admit as a leader this takes up a lot more time, but it's exciting to see people think things out and discover truth.

Roberto was a break-dancer who started coming to our Thursday night service back in 1998. He was a real joker, always clowning around. As I met with him after service and asked him to show me some moves, he asked a lot of spiritual questions. He was pretty skeptical about some things. After about two years of these conversations, he built a relationship with Christ. Hungry to learn more, Rob became our first Bible college student. Shortly after, he got married at Crossover, and today Rob and his family attend and are actively involved.

Each time I prepare a message or a Bible study, I try to put myself in the shoes of my listeners, especially someone new. We get feedback from people, so I can think in advance what questions might be popping up in people's heads and answer them right in the message. In a recent message, I read Colossians 2:6, which

The best yet ■ it now reaches the privacy of your home via the internet ■ it's a spiritual threat ■ it's torn millions to shreds

says, "As you received Christ Jesus the Lord, so walk in him" (ESV). I shared that the word Lord is not a word we commonly use today, and that it means "leader" or "director." I asked the audience if they wondered how we walk with Jesus or why the Bible uses the term walk. I shared that making Jesus your leader is not a sit-down thing. You can't just chill on the couch, clutching the remote. You have to get up and roll, because it's a journey. As we walk through life with Jesus, he also wants us to accomplish several things along the way. By making the message conversational, asking the crowd and myself several questions, dialog occurs as I present the answers. This approach engages a questioning culture.

Questioning can be a beautiful thing, but it can also wear at your patience when leaders question things that they previously accepted as fact or truth. Things they even advocated for earlier may become a gray area because they claim that their situation has changed. I've journeyed through some rough waters with different members and leaders in conversations, as some of them got it and others didn't. One thing to remember is that sometimes the questioning is really an excuse not to accept truth, even if people know it's true. So always pray that God will guide you through these opportunities.

WHO MADE YOU BOSS?

Authority is not popular today. Most people in postmodern emerging generations have a difficult time with it. Hip-hop culture takes this attitude to the next level. The music has always been a vivid form of expression. But as time passed, people pushed the boundaries as they expressed their oppression, grudges, and uncensored opinions. Like rock and roll and R&B, hip-hop has had a rebellious edge, most notably challenging authority—police, teachers, parents, bosses, and even the government. These generations are not scared to call you out or tell you how they feel. Nobody is sacred or untouchable.

On September 2, 2005, Grammy Award–winning hip-hop superstar Kanye West delivered a verbal shot heard around the world. He was one of several celebrities and singers participating in the Concert for Hurricane Relief, a live telethon produced by NBC. Paired up with comedian Mike Myers, he had to read a scripted segment encouraging the American public to make contributions to relief efforts. Kanye abandoned the script on the teleprompter and bad-mouthed the government. His famous closing line was, "George Bush does not care about black people." The audience was stunned. How could he? But many hip-hoppers and people in emerging generations across America raised their fists in approval. It was questioning authority at its finest. The media frowned on his statements, but he gained even more fans. His new album was released the following week and set new records.

Even with all the musical and cultural influences, much of the challenging of authority goes back to family life. There has been a serious breakdown in the American family. In some urban communities, it's well above 60 percent. We also have to factor in emotionally absent fathers. Some fathering advocates say that every social ill faced by America's children

It's got more in bondage than hip-hop's got heads ▪ no DNA threads ▪ no income, no race, no genealogy ▪ see all types of men and women have fallen victim to pornography

is related to fatherlessness. Research shows that children from fatherless homes are more likely to be poor, become involved in drug or alcohol abuse, drop out of school, and suffer from health and emotional problems. Boys are more likely to become involved in crime, and girls are more likely to become pregnant as teens.

God designed the family structure to include both a father and a mother. Although some argue that this model is outdated, they can't argue with the overwhelming data that shows negative results when that family structure deconstructs. One big aspect is the lack of male leadership in so many homes. For decades, women have tried to fill both roles as they raise their kids. Although many have done an incredible job, it's impossible to fill both roles. Recently, my associate pastor and I had to do an intervention with a single mom and her three sons because one of them had questioned his sexual orientation. The reinforcement of a male role model was needed in this situation. A spiritual family needs to step in and fill those gaps. We can't fill a father's shoes, but we can provide some male leadership for young men growing up without a dad.

Fatherlessness breeds a lot of resentment and mistrust in children, resulting in clouded views on authority and leadership. Many of the top hip-hop superstars grew up fatherless themselves, and their music expresses anger toward absent fathers. If they have no respect for their own fathers or parents, then how can we expect them to show proper respect to other authorities? As we engage

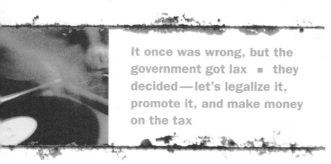

It once was wrong, but the government got lax ▪ they decided—let's legalize it, promote it, and make money on the tax

people in hip-hop culture, we must take into account these underlying attitudes. These individuals may not value the policeman, the politician, or the preacher the way we do, though that shouldn't cause us to shy away from the issue of authority. We even did a three-week message series that focused on submitting to authority and ultimately to God's authority.

LOOK AT ME!

Like several cultures of the past, hip-hoppers want to stick out and show some pride in who they are. They want to be different and distinct. Even in the early days of hip-hop, there was a specific style and flavor to the way people dressed, wore their hair, laced up their sneakers, and wore their hats.

Some take style to extreme levels to get noticed. Baggy clothes have been popular in hip-hop for a while, but styles evolve and change to stay fresh. Recently shorts have become so long that they almost look like pants, and T-shirts are so long that they sometimes reach people's knees. It is not necessarily bad if someone dresses like this. It's just style and an identity. But with some people, it gets out of balance when they always focus on how they look or try to be something they're not. There have been a few people at our church who always try to impress people with their new outfits, new sneakers, or new hairstyles. They try too hard. They've bought into the materialistic mindset, or what some call the ghetto mentality. These people with the nice clothes are the same ones who get evicted, get their cell phones cut off, and don't have any money for food or gas—but they have some new $150 sneakers! It's way out of balance. It's not just single people either. Sometimes it's married people with kids. I've had to sit down with several people and help them make a budget and build some discipline in their lives.

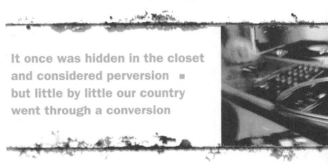

It once was hidden in the closet and considered perversion ■ but little by little our country went through a conversion

Mainstream hip-hop has become a flashy materialistic culture in which superstars flaunt their stuff every chance they get. It's moved to a ridiculous level as nearly every other music video features artists flashing hundred-dollar bills and diamonds or riding in their $300,000 luxury sports cars. Advertisements, TV shows, and movies also push this lavish lifestyle. Our culture is more image-driven than ever. Teens and younger adults especially are vulnerable to this false depiction of happiness. It's why the counterfeit market has exploded in the past few years. Ladies can't afford to buy that three-hundred-dollar Gucci purse, so they get one from the street vendor for twenty, and most people can never tell the difference. Fellows who can't afford a three-thousand-dollar Rolex can get one downtown for twenty. It's funny to see people wearing fake jewelry and diamonds so they can try to look important.

New York City Comptroller William C. Thomas stated in a recent report, "People in NYC paid an estimated $23 billion for counterfeit goods in 2003. Approximately 17 million illegal sound recordings made their way to the streets of NYC for sale to the public."[23] Goldsec.com, a website that tracks counterfeit seizures and activities across the globe, says, "It is estimated that 7 percent of the world trade is in counterfeit goods worth $350 billion." That's a lot of deceit! I wrote a song about this called "Street Vendors":

People want to be something they're not,
buy something they couldn't really afford so they can look hot.

Materialism has flooded hip-hop
and it's not just your local block
but it's the whole rest of society.
You got all these people trying to be
a different person.
Whether you're a businessman, a hip-hop head, or a dude into
    surfing,
your clothes don't make you.
What you got don't shape you.
Be real, be yourself, don't let the mainstream rape you.

Everyday people in hip-hop culture buy into the wrong things, and it destroys their lives slowly but surely.

VISUAL LEARNERS

It's obvious our society is media-driven. With the digital revolution, technology is rapidly changing and becoming more available to everyone. The emerging generations use these newer gadgets before their parents even know what they're called. The internet has become a visual pipeline for information, knowledge, and learning, expanding to phones and laptops with their own wireless satellite links. The latest version of the iPod uploads movies and music videos. Radio and TV shows stream live through the internet. Eventually, they say we will have one gadget that contains all of this technology. As technology changes, it changes our culture as well.

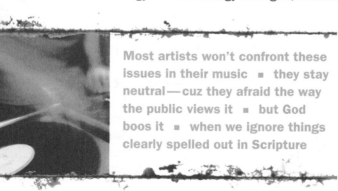

Most artists won't confront these issues in their music ■ they stay neutral — cuz they afraid the way the public views it ■ but God boos it ■ when we ignore things clearly spelled out in Scripture

Media affects people of all ages to some extent. It fuels the materialistic consumer-driven mentality. Even our attention spans are affected as the content and speed of commercials have changed. Frame changes have increased dramatically, with the result that a commercial now flashes a lot more scenes and graphics into the same thirty- or sixty-second slot. Not to mention so many of us now have hundreds of channels to surf during a commercial break. Technology will deliver images and messages more quickly and frequently, bombarding our culture many times more with a worldview contrary to Christianity.

DRUGS AND CRIME

Not everyone influenced by hip-hop is on drugs or doing crime. But when you try reaching this culture, you will run into lots of situations that you wouldn't often run into in traditional or even contemporary ministry. A lot of mainstream hip-hop glorifies selling drugs and drug use, like smoking marijuana, commonly referred to as weed. I've had many conversations with people who don't believe smoking weed is wrong, even people who have been coming to church for a while. They're so rooted in the culture and in the habit, they don't want to give it up and admit that it's wrong. It frequently comes up that God made the plants and that weed is natural for us, so it's really okay. My response is that Scripture tells us we are to obey the

But nowadays the world and the church is one big mixture ▪ step back and look at the big picture, let's face reality ▪ God loves all people but still hates the sin of homosexuality

laws of the land, and last I checked, weed is illegal. The Bible also tells us that we are supposed to take care of our temple (our body), and it's proven that weed will burn a lot of brain cells every time you smoke it. Weed can be an addictive drug. I just emailed a guy who comes around to our church now and then. He'd love to get more involved but has an addiction to weed that he feels he just can't let go of. We continue to pray for brothers and sisters like him.

We've also had several people attend our church who had serious addictions to harder drugs like cocaine and heroine. I've sat and cried with some of these guys or received phone calls late at night from their wives or families as they fall back and go out on a binge. The key thing is that the person must be willing to do whatever it takes to overcome it. Many times they say they are ready, but they really don't want to follow through. Several members of our church are part of Celebrate Recovery, a Christ-centered version of the Twelve-Step Program. Each guy has a sponsor who keeps him accountable daily, and they also attend several meetings each week. Recently, a brother was really struggling with his drug addiction. He almost landed back in jail because he violated probation. But he gave it all up to God and got fully involved in Celebrate Recovery, sharing his testimony in a detox center about how he had been clean for over ninety days. God is into doing miracles. Sometimes we just have to let him do his thing. We've seen several people get cleaned up and restored. Drug addiction is an area that you must be aware of, and you should set up a support system in-house or know who to refer people to if they struggle in these areas.

Drug dealing can be another issue. Over the years, I've lost several teenagers to this trade; most of them are locked up and some of them are dead. When we started our youth ministry, most of our teens came from the housing project in the neighborhood. The streets always buzzed with drug dealers, and there was a steady flow of cars coming into the hood to buy. Many of our teens were twelve or thirteen years old. As they hit fourteen and fifteen, they would be recruited by some of the drug dealers to do runs for them. Soon we'd notice their dwindling church attendance. Eventually, they'd stop coming. Every time we'd go to find them, they'd never be home. Their guardian would tell us that the streets got them. Making several hundred dollars in one day can be very attractive to a teen-ager, especially teenagers who don't have much. This is a hard mentality to break when they know working hard at a fast-food place all week would bring in the same or less amount of money. Plus, the way many hip-hop songs glorify it makes it even more attractive. Be realistic and understand that when someone gets caught up in this lifestyle, it's hard to bring them back to reality. Sometimes it takes an arrest or a shooting to wake them up, but other times it just takes some-

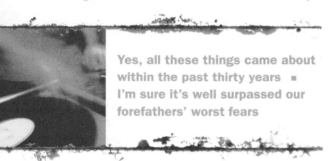

Yes, all these things came about within the past thirty years ∎ I'm sure it's well surpassed our forefathers' worst fears

one reaching out and showing them they care. Our ministry has seen many former drug dealers turn their lives over to Christ and live fruitful lives as we help them find jobs and learn a legal trade.

Several artists talk about the jail time they've done, and this glorifies the experience to some who hear it. To some teens and young adults, going to jail or juvenile detention can even be a badge of honor, giving them more street credibility. I usually find myself in court a couple of times every year as I'm called upon to be a character witness for members of our church who have turned their lives around but still have to face previous charges. Some of these guys did some serious crimes, from bank heists to major drug charges. In 2005, a brother we were working with closely was facing at least fifteen years for a charge from the year before when he was caught with quite a bit of cocaine in his car. God truly did a miracle in his case. He really had changed, and he was attending church and learning a trade. He ended up just having a year of house arrest, and he was still able to work and move up in his new career.

Court is a very uncomfortable place. I have been able to celebrate with families, and I have had to comfort other families when someone gets locked up for a while. These are really vulnerable times when people need spiritual guidance and advice. Sometimes you might not know what to say, but just being there can really make a difference for people. I always encourage those in trouble with the law to make sure they are doing three important things: working, educating themselves (completing high school or attending college or trade school), and attending church regularly. These are key things to help them stay out of trouble and improve themselves, and these are the things that judges look at to see if that person really is making an effort. I've seen some judges have a lot of mercy on people when they can prove they have these things lined up. Anyone can tell the judge a great sob story, but they hear it every day. They want to see some proof of genuine change.

> But where's all the Christians? now this part hurts ▪ most of them was chillin' in their pews — at church

Many offenders also are required to do community service. If you are a nonprofit organization, you can register to become an official site so people can do hours at your facility. We registered with both the juvenile division and the adult division. Our ministry has gotten quite a bit of work done over the years as we plug in people who need hours to come and help out. Most important, this provides a safe haven for them where a lot of great discipleship and fellowship can come out of the time. Several times teens and adults who come here for community service end up attending the church and serving Christ.

SEXPLOITATION

Sports are no longer America's favorite pastime. Porn is. Porn revenue is now larger than the combined revenue of professional football, baseball, and basketball. U.S. porn revenue even exceeds the combined revenue of ABC, CBS, and NBC. According to Family Safe Media, the porn industry generates a staggering fifty-seven billion dollars worldwide, with over twelve billion in the U.S. alone.[24] There are an estimated 4.2 million porn websites on the internet, over 12 percent of the total number of websites on the web. But internet porn isn't even the new frontier anymore. Much of the new technology being developed is funded by the porn industry. Adult movies are available for download for cell phones and iPods, and millions of new users are connecting with it. As more men, women, and teenagers get addicted to this destructive habit, it impacts our society tremendously.

Sex sells, and hip-hop exploits it better than any other music genre. Hip-hop influences pop culture and vice versa, with sex being a big part of both. Unfortunately, the culture has developed a new short-lived career, the "video girl"—girls who appear in hip-hop videos with hardly any clothes on. It's sad that nearly every video in this genre features girls falling all over the artist or dancing by the pool or in a club. VH1 recently did a documentary interviewing several of these girls. Many of them started out really starstruck and young, but within a few years, their eyes were opened to the abuse. The depiction of women in videos degrades women and gives a lot of young males the wrong outlook on females. At the same time, a lot of young women have a twisted idea of who they are, since they look up to these video girls. Mainstream hip-hop is dominated by males, but the few women who are successful artists fall into using sex as a major selling point too.

All these things were for someone else to deal with—what a tragedy ■ things changed—involvement has been replaced with apathy

Sexuality can be an embarrassing and touchy subject that many parents and many churches really don't want to discuss. We must push past that uncomfortable feeling. In my ministry experience, sex is the number-one issue that will mess people up, distract them, and even lead them to walk away from church. It has broken my heart to see so many talented believers get off track because of being in a relationship that turned impure. I've seen this wreck marriages as well. It is vital that we talk about these hot issues and present the correct perspective. People are bombarded all day with the wrong views about sexuality. If we aren't dialoging with them and sharing a biblical perspective, they may never hear it at all. We need to talk about sex and be transparent about the struggle but at the same time present the hope that Christ offers. Crossover Church has offered small groups, message series, and accountability groups. We can't be naive. Many people really struggle with sex, while many others have such a nonchalant attitude about it. With emerging generations, you can't sidestep sexual issues, because they have become such a huge part of our society.

BE READY

If you feel called to reach out and minister to this culture, you must be prepared to get in the trenches. You will face many obstacles. But God can do some incredible things. When you start effectively reaching out and loving people from this culture, they'll come and open up. Be ready to hear what they have to say. Be prayed up and ready for God to speak to you about some things you've never heard before. Some of it is real serious. Recently after a church service, an eighteen-year-old approached me with a real down look and said he needed to talk to me in private. We walked over to the bleachers outside of our basketball courts, and he tearfully shared that he had shot someone the week before. I wasn't expecting to hear that after church service, but that's the crowd we are reaching. I praise God that he allowed us to create a

> But you say, don't blame me, I didn't do a single thing ▪ Exactly, think about it believers— what will *manana* (tomorrow) bring? 🎵🎵

place where people like this young man could come and feel comfortable to open up. I thank God we got to pour into him, give him counsel, and pray with him.

Don't be naive about what people may be going through. We've had strippers, gang members, homosexuals, and all kinds of outcasts attend our church who wanted to leave those lifestyles. You must be ready to meet these people's needs and set up a support system with accountability. In our earlier years, we saw more people like this slip through the cracks. But as we develop more structure, we are connecting people like this with others who can follow up with them and mentor them. We definitely have a ways to go, but we all must step up and be ready to meet the needs of this hurting culture.

10 Communicating Truth

It's important to learn as much as you can about the culture and the people you are trying to reach. Just as foreign missionaries learn about the language and customs of the people group they will evangelize, we need to take more time to research and observe the culture in America. Too many times, we assume we understand the people right down the block, when really we don't have a clue. The hip-hop culture influences people all around us. Even someone who grew up in the culture can quickly lose touch if they don't remain a student of it. Check out the resources section in the back of this book for resources that can help you stay up with what's going on. There will never come a time when you know it all, but there will come a time to act on what you know.

If you're reading this book, you most likely have a heart to reach people influenced by hip-hop. For many believers, attempting to communicate truth can be a scary thing, especially if we're different from the person we're trying to reach. We need to let God's Spirit guide us and give us the words and the wisdom that only he can provide. In Acts 1:8, Jesus tells us to go out and be his witnesses locally, regionally, and globally. But the great part is that he promises that his Spirit will empower us.

Over ten years ago, I put the knowledge I had gained from experience, research, and college into full-time action at a place called Crossover. I didn't know it all. I still don't. I've had several failures, but also lots of victories. Reaching this culture is like trying to find your way in a maze of obstacles that only God can help you navigate through. I will share in detail what we have learned and how we do ministry at this stage in our journey. We're constantly growing and learning, but we're confident we can share some helpful insights. Hopefully we can help you avoid some of the mistakes we've made, share in some of the victories we've seen, and smash some of the false assumptions we've held in the past.

BUILDING RELATIONSHIPS

Evangelism has to become more of a lifestyle than just an outreach or an event. Unfortunately, many Christians box evangelism into something they do at a certain time, like another activity on their calendar. But when we look in Scripture, evangelism is what we are supposed to be about all the time. This issue can't be addressed only through the sermons; it also needs to be modeled and encouraged among the leaders and the rest of the church family. Evange-lism events can be great things. But if they are not followed up with relation-ships, they usually bring little or no fruit.

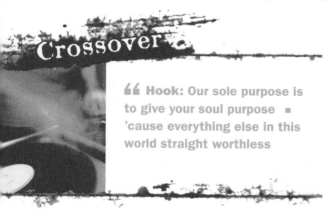

ff Hook: Our sole purpose is to give your soul purpose ▪ 'cause everything else in this world straight worthless

Every weekend, we have several first-time guests in each of our services. We hand out programs that in-clude a feedback card they fill out and turn in. As we research our own audience, we have discovered some interesting things. A section on the feedback card asks first-time guests how they heard about the church. Our church is on public-access cable, which reaches tens of thousands in our city every week. We also have run some commercials locally on MTV and BET, and we usually have thousands of flyers, CDs, and magazines in circulation in the area. Yet most visitors respond to this question by saying they came because of a friend. The flyer, the commercial, or the TV show might have sparked an interest, but it is the personal invitation that got them to actu-ally come.

Relationships are vital in communicating truth to the hip-hop culture. Barna.org states, "Young adults are much more likely to share their faith through ongoing discussions with friends and through email and instant message conversations than are middle-aged and older adults."[25] In 1997, Carlos Ramirez, aka Los-1, attended art school here in Tampa and built a relationship with a guy named Spec. They both were from New York and were into hip-hop. Over the next few months, they got to know each other, and Los let Spec know that he rapped himself. He shared about how he includes a lot of his faith in his music. Immediately, Spec got turned off and even laughed at the idea. Los didn't give up. He still kept building with him and invited him to some of his concerts. But something always seemed to come up, and Spec didn't go until March 1998. Los invited him to a concert at Crossover, where he was the opening act for a CD-release concert for my second CD, *The Answers*. Spec didn't

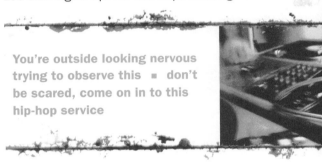

You're outside looking nervous trying to observe this ■ don't be scared, come on in to this hip-hop service

want to go, but out of respect for his friend, he decided to come for a few minutes. He grew up in the Catholic Church, so he thought a hip-hop concert at a church was going to be wack. But when Spec walked in that night, he was floored to see over three hundred people who looked just like him vibing to the music. He came in during the last song of the night and heard me share the story of Christ. Spec had never heard or seen Christianity presented like this, and God's Spirit moved him. He responded to the invitation to receive prayer. He didn't go to the club that night but instead went out to eat with some of us afterward. Although he responded for prayer, he didn't make a commitment that night. It was all new, and he was still processing it.

The following Wednesday, I called Spec and invited him to our Thursday night service. He was tripping that I personally called and reached out to him. The next day, he showed up and rolled with me as I picked up some teens in the church van. That night, at the end of service, he began a relationship with Christ. The next few months, he attended every Thursday and built a relationship with me and several people at the church. After a long weekend of concerts, one Monday morning I awoke to someone frantically pounding on my door. I opened it to find Spec in tears. He told me his mother, sister, and grandmother were in a car accident and he needed me to drive him to the hospital forty-five minutes away. When we arrived, we found out his grandmother had died and his sister and mother were injured badly. He was devastated. I prayed with him and shared a few thoughts, but mostly all I could do was just be there for him. A few weeks later, he left for New York to spend the summer up there and get away from everything. I called to check up on him several times. It was a real testing time for his faith. This is where relationships are key!

Spec came back in the fall and got discipled and more involved. He volunteered his artwork for flyers and graphics for the church. He eventu-

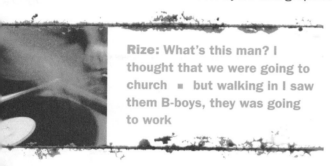

Rize: What's this man? I thought that we were going to church ∎ but walking in I saw them B-boys, they was going to work

ally finished college, and today he works full time at the church as our media director. Our magazines, flyers, album covers, websites, films, and more are all products of his creativity. Spec has become one of my best friends in life, and he has traveled with me to minister at countless events across the country and overseas.

When you see the relationship-building process duplicated, you see even more lasting fruit. Shortly after Spec started coming, he invited Melissa from his workplace. Melissa had no church background and was very skeptical, but she soon built a relationship with Christ. Over the years, she has poured into many teens and adults at the ministry. About a year ago, she invited Bert from her workplace to visit. Eventually, Bert checked it out, and after a few services he began a relationship with Christ. Today, Bert has become actively involved in our media department. He feels he has found his purpose in life and is now going to school to study filmmaking so that in the future he can produce Christ-centered films. When you see true relationships being built and duplicated, you can trace a spiritual genealogy like the one I just shared.

GETTING THE UNCOMMITTED COMMITTED

The meaning of commitment has become very watered down in our society. One thing I admire about previous generations is that they knew what commitment is. We live in a consumer culture in which everyone wants things faster, cheaper, and better. Unfortunately, this mindset has leaked into other areas of our lives, and many people think that nearly everything can be upgraded for something better. Today, people are quick to break commitments at their jobs, in their marriages, in their friendships, and with their personal morals. Some people have never had commitment modeled for them, so the percentage of broken homes continues to rise. Many have become so consumer-minded that if they don't like something, they won't even give it a fair chance. They'll just move on to the next thing, because everything is disposable. People switch jobs, marriages, friends, and churches quicker than ever. Most of the people influenced by hip-hop culture never had a commitment to God or to any church. So it's quite a challenge when the person you are trying to reach asks, "What will it mean if I do accept God?"

Genuine commitment breaks down the free-spirited person who just wants to sleep around, believe what he or she wants, and act on impulse. Past generations went through rebellious phases but eventually came back to the need for commitment. But emerging generations have made noncommitment a lifestyle. Noncommitment isn't countercultural anymore; it's an accepted characteristic of mainstream pop culture, propagated by pop-culture messages. The content of many hip-hop songs is anticommitment at its core.

Once people have built a relationship with Christ, the goal is to move them to maturity as they get plugged into a church. We all know this isn't always an easy task, but it's a necessary thing. A church like ours that is geared to the hip-hop culture especially struggles with this. But don't shy away from asking people for commitment. Commitment is biblical. Ephesians 2:19 says, "Consequently, you are no longer foreigners and strangers, but fellow citizens with God's people and also members of his household." When we become fellow citizens and members, responsibility and commitment come into play. When commitment is modeled and presented in the right way, people see it as attractive and want in on it. Even though our culture can be anticommitment, all of us long for it internally.

> Hearing sounds all around that sound more like a club ▪ not sure what's going on, but yo I'm feeling madd love

At Crossover, we celebrate commitment in many ways, and we ask for it constantly. It starts with asking people to commit their lives to Christ or to commit to grow in certain areas. We have people respond to this every time we offer it in a service. Our speaking teams often weave inspiring stories of commitment into our messages. Once people commit to Christ, we encourage them to check out our connection classes, which are adapted from Saddleback Church.

Beyond these classes, we constantly encourage opportunities for people to serve and get involved—for instance, in small groups. A few times a year, we'll have special events to honor our volunteers and their commitment to serving. These events are complete with meals, games, awards, and lots of appreciation. Several times a year, we have work days at the church, during which members will volunteer their time to remodel, paint, clean, build, and do all kinds of fun things. In the past few years, we have completed tens of thousands of dollars worth of remodeling and building for free as people have volunteered to make our church campus a better place. The beautiful thing about commitment is that it creates ownership. It's no longer just *my* church, as the pastor; now it's *our* church. It's our patio that we built, or our wall with the newly painted mural. Ownership is important to hip-hop culture.

COMMUNITY

Even though younger adults may not like commitment, they are well aware of their deep longing for community and relationships. We are made with a need to belong, and younger adults especially look to connect with something to fill that void. Many of them find it in fraternities, community organizations, club scenes, or even in street gangs. In the past number of years, the internet has become a huge community through chat rooms, message boards, instant messaging, and blogging. The biggest example is MySpace.com, the largest online community in internet history. In less than three years, it has over one hundred million members and is still growing. It has become the place to be for young adults and teens. Their personal pages display pictures, music, and their story, and they reconnect with old friends and meet new people.

> Then praise and worship starts, they got a DJ too ▪ no way that this can be praise to you ▪ then I look around and every eye is closed ▪ cats with their hands in the air and no it's not a pose

People kept asking me if I had a page on the network, especially since a lot of artists are on there to promote their music. I finally got my page up in spring 2006, and tens of thousands have clicked on it. It has been a great ministry tool for me, and I've connected with people from around the world and from my own community. People have emailed my account with lots of encouragement and prayers, while others ask for prayer and encouragement. I've had several teens and young adults reach out as they were going through suicidal thoughts, bad relationships, and questions about their faith. This is a whole new ministry tool that we didn't have a few years ago. But MySpace can also be a very dangerous place if it is not used for the right reasons or monitored. I'm not an advocate for people to have a MySpace page. It's not for everyone. Just like anywhere else on the net, you're only a click away from inappropriate pictures, videos, and language. I know several people who have shut down their pages because it became too much of a temptation. You have to have accountability, and you have to be there for a purpose. As believers, we are called to be salt and light everywhere we go, even in cyberspace!

And they're dressed like me, but I see tears in their eyes ▪ T-shirts and baggy pants, but I see joy in their lives ▪ man I was unsure when I came through the door ▪ but now I want to know a little more

Our church did an entire message series with short films in 2006 that was titled "MySpace: Is God Invited?" The series touched on community, identity, time, and space. We had incredible services as we challenged our people to look at the profile of their lives. More than fifty people built new relationships with Christ, and several people made changes in their lives and their MySpace pages.

MySpace is an indicator of the interest young people have in community. But can this desire be directed to a faith community? Yes! We've seen it happen at Crossover. Our church is filled with people who were not involved in church, but church has now become a major part of who they are. Church has to be more than just a service on the weekends. We provide a variety of things for people to connect with throughout the week. We offer basketball leagues, small groups, talent development classes, skateboarding, community outreach, volunteering, break dancing, and more. For many of our members, the church has truly become their family, and they have never experienced the depth of the relationships they've built now.

WHAT A WORSHIP SERVICE LOOKS LIKE

When people hear that we are a church that targets hip-hop culture, they ask about our church services. I'll get all kinds of crazy questions like, "Do you rap your sermons?" or, "Do you guys read and study the Bible, or are your services mostly just entertainment?" They may be funny, but honestly, some of these questions can be somewhat offensive. But I put myself in other people's shoes, since many are clueless when it comes to the culture. We know God has called us to build bridges and educate others. Crossover's worship services have many elements that any Christian church might have: singing, prayer, an offering, announcements, a message, and special music. But the way we do these things is definitely different. We're obviously not traditional, but everything we believe and practice in our services is biblical. Remember, Jesus was not a traditional guy! As a matter of fact, he was constantly in conflict with the religious leaders of his day because he kept challenging them. In Matthew 23, he stresses how they looked good on the outside and put on a great show, but their insides were rotten. One comment we constantly hear about our services is how real they are. Although they are professional, well prepared, and well thought out, they are open and honest. Hip-hop culture wants realness.

If you were to walk into one of our weekend services, you'd find we welcome everyone and start off in prayer as we lead into worship. Music is a huge element with our crowd, so our worship style reflects our cultural context. We have a DJ on turntables spinning a Christian hip-hop or R&B instrumental. Our worship team sings many of the same songs other churches do, but with a remixed flavor. A rapper or two will mix in on some of the faster songs and rap a verse between repetitions of the chorus. The worship team will also sing some slower songs with R&B ballads, sing a capella, or sing with someone beat-boxing in the background. People authentically engage in worship with God. They clap, raise their hands, cry, sway side to side, or sit quietly.

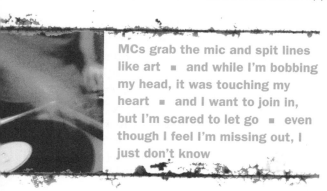

MCs grab the mic and spit lines like art ▪ and while I'm bobbing my head, it was touching my heart ▪ and I want to join in, but I'm scared to let go ▪ even though I feel I'm missing out, I just don't know

Worship is more than just singing. We see this in Scripture, but many churches box it into only singing. At many services, we'll mix in rap, poetry, Scripture reading, and occasionally dance or an artist painting a mural during the slow reflective songs. Our worship team (Harmony) has also written several songs. They've produced several CDs complete with instrumentals so they can be used as a resource by other churches.

We never use secular beats at our services, because we've found that it only brings confusion. Some contemporary churches may do cover songs and incorporate secular rock music, but with hip-hop culture, I'd really encourage you to think twice, pray, and get godly counsel. When we first incorporated turntables into worship at our youth service in 1998, we occasionally used a popular secular beat that was on the radio. We found mixed reactions. Many times the crowd would seem to get into it more, but as we looked closer, some people were singing the other words. Music can bring a different spirit into the room, especially when people know the other words behind it. Most mainstream hip-hop promotes a message totally op-posite from what we give. The clincher for us was when teens and young adults asked the leaders why we played these beats. These were unchurched youth from the culture who were now trying to serve God. They tried to stop listening to this music, but then they'd walk into church and hear the

Will they judge me cause I've done so much? ■ but still I long to feel God's touch ■ can I change man, 'cause I've gone so far ■ then I hear them say come as you are (as you are)

instrumental being played. These teens and young adults from the housing projects and the neighborhood felt it wasn't right. We soon stopped using any secular beats. As we built up our arsenal of Christian vinyl and CD in-strumentals, we now have plenty of instrumentals to choose from.

We generally create a time after worship when people say what's up to each other and say hello to new people. Dead air is always awkward, so we always have our DJ on the tables playing a backdrop instrumental during these times and during announcements to keep the atmosphere upbeat. Hip-hoppers are visual learners, so we keep this in mind as we present the message. Some churches may tie in special music, drama, or a video at the beginning or the end of a message. I encourage you to mix it into your message at several different points to illustrate your theme and the Scripture you share. The reality is that our attention spans have become short, and for younger genera-tions, it's even shorter. It may seem like an obstacle, but it doesn't have to be. Our average message is

Now it's time for open mic, I hear the DJ say ■ 'bout twenty MCs rush the stage, but I look away ■ 'cause my boy told me that Christian rap was weak ■ their flows are all cheesy plus they use whack beats

still around thirty-five to forty minutes long, but we tie in other elements at different points to keep the crowd engaged. Many times we provide notes in our programs so they can follow along and take additional notes. Our media team produces some innovative graphics on the screens to illus-trate certain points and display some of the Scriptures we read together.

The layout of our service constantly changes because we want to be predictably unpredictable. We don't want it to become routine. Sometimes, we may do a slower worship set after the message, or do an offering right in the middle of worship. Our average service is around seventy-five to eighty minutes long. We plan services together as a team, so there are many people and many creative elements involved. We've found it necessary to put together a programming sheet so everyone can be on the same page in all of the different areas. But we aren't stuck on the exact times, since sometimes God will redirect things. We believe that God is pleased when we plan ahead and that his Spirit is involved when we are putting the services together. (See appendix 1 for a sample programming sheet.)

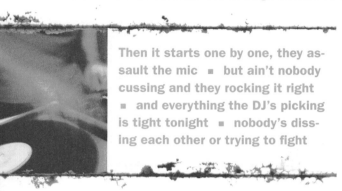

Then it starts one by one, they assault the mic ■ but ain't nobody cussing and they rocking it right ■ and everything the DJ's picking is tight tonight ■ nobody's dissing each other or trying to fight

MESSAGE SERIES

Many pastors and youth pastors don't have any idea about the message they will share in their services a month from now, or even a week from now. A frequent statement you'll hear is that they want to be led by the Spirit from week to week. I used to operate like this myself in the early years of my youth ministry. But when you roll like this, many times you end up addressing a current problem while still feeling the pressure of putting out a fire from a previous dilemma. A lot of times, it's not truly being led by the Spirit. It's more like being led by a lack of organization and planning. God does have mercy on us and can still use us. But when we plan ahead, God can help us take things to the next level.

In the past several years at Crossover, we have done things different when it comes to messages. In the process, we've really discovered what works with our audience. During our weekly staff meeting, we'll frequently ask what our team is observing among people at the church, outside the church, and in the culture as a whole. From these responses and from others in the church, our pastoral team will prayerfully decide what some of the big emerging issues are. Some issues we need to address again. We creatively tie in these issues or themes with Scripture and with the culture to get people's attention. Then, our pastoral team will generally have the titles and direction of message series for four to six months.

Message series can build momentum if you set up each week to flow into the next one in order to reach a climax. Several of our message series have had an original short film or a drama that continued each week. Our services and series are fun and engaging, but they always end up with a serious challenge each week. Sex is a big issue that our culture struggles with, and many times the church is pretty quiet about it. We did a series called "Sex in the Church? Yes, We Need to Talk!" It was a candid series that dealt with lust, pornography, relationships, and ultimately God's plan for sex. Many people got accountable and made changes in their lives and in their relationships.

In 2006, we did a series called "Reasonable Doubt: What Does the Evidence Prove?" Our flyer had a picture of the *Mona Lisa* from *The DaVinci Code* book and movie to grab people's attention. With all the different ideas about Christ flying around in society, we felt we needed to present the truth. It was an in-depth series looking at the evidence for the Bible's historical accuracy and for the life, death, and resurrection of Christ. We followed that up with a series on 1 Corinthians titled "If We Are the Church, Then We Should ..." a message series that dug into the issues that Paul dealt with in the church in Corinth. So much of it is relevant to today, and much of the content surprised many people who haven't read much Scripture.

In the rules they said you had to rep Christ ■ and they do it ease like it's in their lives ■ now the last man grabs the mic, I think his name's Urban D.

We've done series on pain, purpose, finances, and community, among several others. We even did a series on the Ten Commandments. We called it "The Creator's Top 10" and made it like a music-video countdown format each week. I encourage you to plan ahead and plan with a team. Be real and talk about the issues that people are dealing with. The church needs to address the hot topics of culture from a biblical standpoint. (For more message ideas and resources, see appendix 2.)

CAMPUS DESIGN

Architecture is language. What is your church facility saying to people when they arrive? I know that finances can be a barrier, but some inexpensive improvements like paint and lighting can do wonders. It's all about perceived value. You may have an older church building that you think you can't do much with. You're wrong! There's always potential. Our main auditorium at Crossover was built in 1958, and our offices and additional classroom space were built in 1970. It's got some years to it. The electrical was outdated, the ceilings are low, and we even had termite and water damage. If you had seen it about four or five years ago, you would never have thought it would be a place to house an innovative ministry like ours. Since then, it has been transformed. Being a visionary, God showed me pieces of the puzzle of how we could make the Crossover campus more functional and more attractive. As I travel to other ministries in other cities, I'm constantly observing their facilities, along with restaurants, malls, movie theaters, and other places people commonly spend time. I'm constantly looking for new ideas.

For the past few years, there has been a conversation about the emerging church and what many younger adults are looking for. Many will share that younger adults want an old-looking vintage church building with stained-glass windows and crosses. This is true for people in certain parts

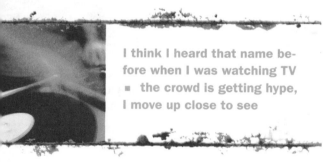

I think I heard that name before when I was watching TV ▪ the crowd is getting hype, I move up close to see

of the country and in more suburban environments. But it's different in urban communities. Although most hip-hoppers don't attend church, nearly all of them have gone to a few services at some point in their lives. Services in traditional buildings bring back memories of boring or bad experiences. We've found that for our audience, a vintage-type setting is a huge turnoff. It brings back uncomfortable memories of sitting in a pew with their grandmother, dressed up in a suit and tie or a dress and sitting there for three hours. Most churches have moved away from pews, which is a good thing for people in hip-hop culture. What are the only two places in their cultural context where there are pews? Church and court. Many people in our congregation have been in court for themselves or their family or friends. It's not a comfortable place to be. If you have pews in your facility and you're trying to reach this culture, I suggest that the pews should go, since they create a barrier.

We've found that people who visit our church and even people who attend our church constantly comment that the place doesn't look like a regular church. It's very different. It's important to create space for people to be able to hang out and fellowship. Relationships are important, so you need to provide some areas for them to happen. People in hip-hop culture love to hang out and eat. When I took over as pastor in 2002, I knew we needed to create a nice area for people to hang out with each other. After church, everyone stood around outside in the dirt by the parking lot. It was ghetto! We built a patio right outside our entrance with simple patio blocks. As we grew, we created more space by adding some awnings, a food-service counter, restaurant booths, an information area, lighting, and TV monitors. Today, the patio seats over 125 people and serves as an incredible meeting area where a lot of great ministry happens. In Florida, we can use this all year round.

We also created a full-court basketball court and a ten-thousand-square-foot skate park. Private donors and local foundations gave us grants to fund these dreams, which we had for years. We learned to be patient and wait on God's timing.

He's freestyling 'bout the crowd, and now he's looking at me ■ and yo the next thing I know, he's talking 'bout my shirt ■ and he don't even know me, I don't go to this church

Crossover has a small auditorium that seats only just over two hundred people, so we've had to be creative with our space. On the back of the church, we added an outdoor overflow seating patio with a big awning and fans. We recently added temporary walls that can slide into place so we can use a newly installed air-conditioning system during the hotter summer months. Lighting creates mood. Emerging generations like it to be dark during a worship service. We installed soft recessed lighting with dimmers throughout the auditorium. No more bright white florescent lights! It made the auditorium feel softer and relaxing, more like a big living room. We found that the crowd became much more receptive during worship when it was dimmer. We turn the lights up during the message so people can read their Bibles and take notes. And the stage has several colored gel lights that illuminate the speaker. The audience doesn't feel like everyone is staring at them, so they feel freer to participate. In his book *The Emerging Church*, Dan Kimball writes, "Perhaps in some way the whole concert scene, where the lights go out and the band plays, has had some influence on emerging generations' desire for a sense of darkness in worship."[26] I would agree this is the case with hip-hoppers.

Art is also language. Our entire campus is filled with creativity and customization. Several artists from our church have painted and airbrushed murals on several of the walls and patio tabletops. We also recently installed several light boxes on our patio and in our main auditorium on all the walls. These resemble the kind you'll see at movie theaters or

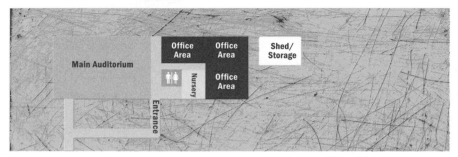

Original configuration of Crossover

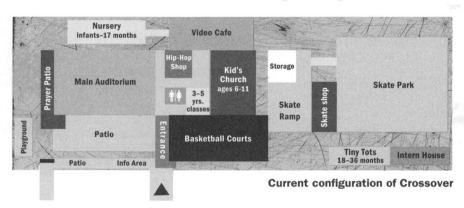

Current configuration of Crossover

airports. They are filled with urban scenes with Scripture verses and graffiti-style artwork. We even have a triangular backlit sign at the entrance of our patio with a campus map on one side and advertisements on the other side for upcoming concerts and events at Crossover. When people step on our campus and see the raw creativity presented in a professional way, it speaks volumes both to our own people as well as to visitors who are interested in what we are about.

Our small lobby has a hip-hop shop with more than ninety CDs, along with magazines, Bibles, books, T-shirts, and DVDs. We even have listening stations on the wall so people can listen to the CDs before they buy them. When hip-hoppers see these things, it excites them because they see that spirituality can be tied in with real life and familiar things. It communicates to them that Christianity doesn't have to be boring and outdated, as many of them had previously viewed it. The past number of years, our campus has been constantly evolving. In the diagrams, you can see what was original and what has been added since 2002. There's really nothing more we can add now, as we are totally out of space, but it's been a great learning process, and we're much better equipped to design our next campus when we relocate in the future.

PRAYER

Neither our personal ministry nor our church's ministry will get very far without prayer. We must spend time with our Father to get equipped, refreshed, and inspired. We'll quickly run out of steam without prayer. But we must remember prayer is not just for us as we present our needs. In Scripture, we see that there are gratitude, thankfulness, and praise elements to this conversation, something we forget or rush through in our prayer time. If we take time to listen to our prayer life, it can sound pretty self-centered. It might sound like the person who calls only

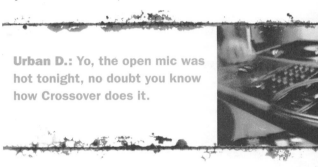

Urban D.: Yo, the open mic was hot tonight, no doubt you know how Crossover does it.

when they need something. When we see their name pop up on caller ID, we roll our eyes because we don't have a genuine relationship with them. They're calling us only for what they can get from us. How do we sound in our "calls" to our creator?

Prayer has always played a role in our ministry. I'd love to be able to say that it's always been at the forefront, but that wouldn't be true. Our prayer ministry has gone through its ups and downs over the years. Leaders and volunteers have changed quite a bit as we've tried to figure out what would work best in our cultural context. Anytime the building is open during the week, we let our members know they can stop by and pray if they desire. It happens several times a week with different individuals.

But we also wanted to make some times when people can gather. Occasionally, we'll have a prayer night. But we've found this is hard for people to commit to regularly because so many are working and overcommitted. So we have formed a prayer team that prays during each

If everybody could take their seats we're gonna get into the Word tonight. We're gonna talk about what it means to have a real relationship with Christ.

service in our prayer area. Members of the team attend one service and pray during the other. They pray for the leadership of the church, upcoming events, prayer requests sent to us via email and mail, and some of the feedback cards from our services that contain prayer requests and praise reports.

Our staff also meets weekly to pray for feedback-card requests and to share personal requests. This also helps our staff keep in touch with the needs and praise reports of our people. It's quite humbling as our hearts are broken from the requests. Yet at the same time, our hearts are filled with joy for the many answered prayers.

If possible, it's important to create a space specifically for prayer. We previously had a room upstairs in the back of the building, but we found this wasn't very effective. Most people didn't know where it was, and some weren't comfortable going to this unknown room after they responded in a service. So we created a conveniently located space for prayer in a common area. We call it the prayer patio. It's on the far end of the patio, where it wraps around the front side of the building to give it some privacy. After services, we tell people that if they want prayer for anything they can stop by the prayer patio to talk with someone. If they need a Bible or a devotional, they can stop by the prayer patio. This is a place where we can connect and follow up with them. We've been excited to see fruit from this space.

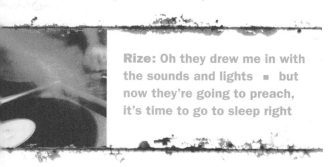

Rize: Oh they drew me in with the sounds and lights ∎ but now they're going to preach, it's time to go to sleep right

COMMUNICATION TOOLS

Communicating your vision and promoting your ministry have to go beyond just what can be shared verbally in your services. Image is important. Some will say that emerging generations don't care about image when it comes to church and will shy away from things that look professional. But for the hip-hop culture, image is important, though we don't want our church's image to appear too corporate or too disconnected from hip-hop. At Crossover, we put a lot of emphasis on excellence, but still with our authentic flavor. We've created several communication tools that share our vision in print, web, CD, and DVD.

As people arrive on our campus, the design, the murals, and the large backlit posters communicate what we are about. When they walk into the auditorium, they are handed a full-color glossy program designed with some cutting-edge artwork. For many visitors, the program communicates, "Wow, this is a hot program. I've never seen anything like this. These people are up on their game." Most hip-hoppers think church is going to be corny, outdated, or cheesy. These tools begin to smash those stereotypes.

Since we're such a unique church, we found that first-time guests frequently asked a lot of questions or walked away wondering what we were really about. When I took over as pastor, we tried to figure out some kind of communication piece to let people know about us. After brainstorming, we decided to create a magazine. In 2003, we developed our first annual church magazine, which we give out to all first-time guests. Our magazine has grown in size from twenty-four pages to up to one hundred pages. We got ads from several Christian music labels and people who believed in us, which helped pay for a good chunk of the printing. Several colleges, resource companies, publishing companies, and music labels now partner with us as our ministry has grown in visibility. Ads continue to pay for most of the printing costs, and we're able to give away the magazine to thousands who visit throughout the year.

The magazine contains our history, statement of faith, staff member bios, information about the programs and services we offer, and several testimonies and articles on faith and culture. It's developed into a magazine that rivals the quality of any urban magazine. It is definitely one of our best communication tools. I am the publisher and one of the writers. Our staff and volunteers do all the writing and editing. Our full-time graphic designer at the church seems to take it to the next level each time. It takes a lot of time and effort, but we've found it is well worth it. We eventually branded the magazine under the name *SOUL Mag* (Speaking on Urban Life), available through our website. I believe this communication strategy can work quite well for any church, since you can tailor your magazine to your audience.

Not only does each first-time guest get a magazine, but later we mail them a free CD of the music of several artists from Crossover and the testimonies of several of our members. DJ Lopez is a member of our church who takes all the music and

> But when he spoke, yo it was real, he wasn't being a fake
> ■ I think there's some decisions for me to make

testimonies and puts them together in a mix CD format so everything flows seamlessly. The mix CD style has been very popular in hip-hop for several years. It's a great ministry piece, since the final track shares the gospel in detail. Over the past few years, we've raised money to press up nearly ten thousand CDs, and it has impacted our community as a great evangelism tool. It also serves as a great opportunity to support our in-house artists and help them get their music out. Lopez recently put together our fifth volume of this CD series, which we call the Crossover Cypha.

Websites are another vital communication tool. Chris Chatman is a lay-person in our church who came alongside Spec and did an incredible job developing our church site. The site has a wealth of information about the church, including upcoming messages, guest artists, news, and resources. In 2005, our Crossover Church and Fla.vor Alliance websites collectively received over 3.6 million hits. Developing an email list through your website is a no-brainer. We collect email addresses from our feedback cards and enter them into our database. There is also a place on our website where people can sign up. Don't overdo sending emails, or people will treat them like spam. We generally send out only one or two emails a month so that people will actually read them.

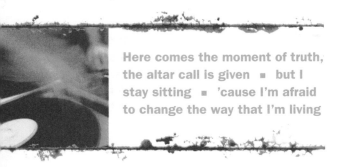

Here comes the moment of truth, the altar call is given ■ but I stay sitting ■ 'cause I'm afraid to change the way that I'm living

CREATIVE PROMOTIONS

You might do some phenomenal stuff at your church, but if you don't have some creative ways to get the word out, you'll fall short of your maximum impact. My first piece of promotional advice is, "Don't use cheese, or you'll be disappointed with the results!" For example, don't produce flyers on full pages of paper on your copy machine. Due to lack of knowledge and money, we used to do this, and we quickly found out that people didn't take it seriously. Even though we had a great concert coming up, the flyer communicated that it was another poorly put-together Christian event. Quarter-page flyers have been one of our greatest and most afford-able tools, since they resemble the type of full-color flyers that clubs and concerts use. People take them to work, school, and everywhere they roll. They can also be used for direct mail. We even have a street team that goes to certain events and uses them to promote the church and upcom-ing services and events.

Public access TV can be another affordable avenue for promotion. Many cable providers make this available for free if people go through the training and pass the tests. We have a dedicated couple in our church who put our services into the system each week. People actually check those stations out as they channel surf. According to people at the station, our service became one of the best shows on public access due to its unique-ness. Several people joined the church as a result of watching it on public access.

You don't have to be a megachurch to advertise on TV. We have run some commercials, produced by our media team, on MTV and BET through our cable provider, Bright House, which reaches over two hundred thousand homes in the city of Tampa and the rest of Hillsborough County. That's some serious local coverage. We chose to run them a few times a day during the peak hours between 4:30 and 7:30 p.m., during highly rated shows like *Rap City*, *106 and Park*, *Made*, and *TRL*. How much does this cost? Our average thirty-second commercial at peak hours in 2006 was just under fifteen dollars per slot. These spots have produced some great results, not necessarily by attracting big numbers by themselves but as a deciding factor for many to finally visit after being invited several times. The ads bring a new level of awareness when our people talk to others about the church and give them a flyer. Several have responded something like, "Oh, I heard about that on BET! Yeah, I've been meaning to check that out, but I didn't know where it was." These commercials have also brought extra traffic to our website, since the web address is displayed throughout the commercial.

Doing big things doesn't always cost big money!

BUILDING MINISTRIES AROUND THE VISION

It's important to establish your vision and mission with clarity. In 2002, our leadership prayerfully concluded that our mission is "to relevantly introduce the truth of Christ to the hip-hop culture as we develop worship, purpose, unity, and leadership in their lives." We stated that our intent is to implement the five purposes of the New Testament church—evangelism, worship, ministry, fellowship, and discipleship—in a relevant way for the hip-hop culture. There are always

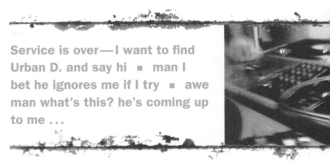

Service is over—I want to find Urban D. and say hi ∎ man I bet he ignores me if I try ∎ awe man what's this? he's coming up to me ...

people eager to start up new ministries at churches, but sometimes they don't fit with where the church is headed. The danger is that people in these ministries can become their own entity and create their own agenda for the direction of the whole church. It can get ugly. Even back in Crossover's early days, people had their own ideas of where the church should go, since our vision was so broad and the church was floundering. During 2002, it became clearer where the church was headed after we established our mission statement.

When you are just starting a church of this type, or transitioning a small church, act your age! Admit to people that you will not be able to offer everything overnight. It takes time to develop solid children's and youth ministries with dependable leaders and volunteers. It takes time to develop a solid discipleship program and small groups. Don't be afraid to tell people that you're not there yet. On the other hand, while keeping the balance, you want to push to get things going. But be careful that you never start a ministry without a qualified person to lead it. One of our biggest problems in our earlier years was a lack of solid leaders, since we had so many new believers. Even though we've grown and have developed a good team, we need to constantly raise up more leaders to duplicate themselves, or our growth will slow to a halt.

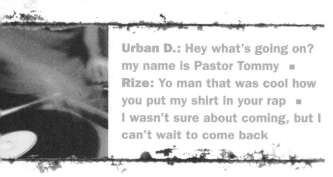

Urban D.: Hey what's going on? my name is Pastor Tommy ▪ **Rize:** Yo man that was cool how you put my shirt in your rap ▪ I wasn't sure about coming, but I can't wait to come back

We categorize each of our ministries by one of the five purposes of the New Testament church: evangelism, worship, ministry, fellowship, or discipleship. When someone comes up with an idea for a new ministry, we see if it would fit into one of these purposes and make sure it's culturally relevant for our target audience. For example, a knitting ministry will not work with our crowd! You have to learn to say no sometimes. But when your vision is clear and everything flows with it, you rarely run into occasions when people don't get it. Of course, people will have their own agendas for a number of reasons, from doctrine to ministry to wanting power and attention. We've almost always found that such individuals come from other churches with their cultural church baggage. There have been a few extreme incidents when our pastoral council asked people to no longer fellowship with us, since they created so much disruption. We never want it to get to that point. But in some cases, you must enforce church discipline when people are not respecting authority. On a good note, some of those people eventually were restored.

In order for someone to start a new ministry at our church, they have to go through our connection classes, plus put together a proposal that our staff and pastoral council can look at and pray about. If it fits in with the vision and they have proven themselves to be solid leadership material, we make plans to implement their proposal and get their ministry started. For example, we started an outreach ministry called Filaments of Truth, which focuses on poetry and spoken word. It also incorporates rapping, singing, and sharing testimonies. A brother in the church had it in his heart to gather up some of the talent in the church and take it to the streets, other venues, and other churches. He put together an incredible proposal that blew us away. He even built a website and had flyer and T-shirt designs already set up. The time and effort he had put into it showed his seriousness. His proposal has become a model for others who desire to spark something off. Since he had served in other areas and several of the staff had spent time with him, we knew he had integrity. The team has grown to close to twenty people, and it has been exciting to hear their stories.

DISCOVERING, DEVELOPING, AND DISPLAYING TALENT AND PASSION

We've had many people walk through our doors who felt they didn't have any purpose. In the process of finding Christ and getting involved, they discovered purpose and areas they were gifted in. We've also had many people walk through our doors with talent and passion who didn't know Christ. As they built a relationship with him, they needed new outlets in which to channel their gifts and to be discipled. It's important that you create avenues for people to discover, develop, and display their talents and passions.

Several years ago, we started our weekly talent development classes. Since we already had several rappers, singers, and dancers attending our church, numerous teens and young adults expressed a desire

Urban D.: Yo I'm glad you got the chance to come ▪ it's nice to meet you ▪ your accent sounds up north—yo where you from? ▪ **Rize:** The Bronx New York

to learn how to do those things. We also had a group of people who could do those things and had a relationship with Christ but needed some discipleship. It's also important to encourage those who are solid and talented to give back and pour into others.

The MC class is for those who want to learn how to rap or rap better. The class is run by members of Fla.vor Alliance who have all recorded several of their own CDs, traveled, and had experience in the music industry. Teens and adults in our church really look up to these guys as role models. The MC class teaches the history of hip-hop, developing song concepts, writing techniques, expanding your vocabulary, freestyling, stage presence, studio recording, and how the industry really runs. If the class members complete the twelve-week semester, they get to record a song in a real studio, and they get an opportunity to perform in our services.

Our DJ and production class is led by some of our in-house DJs who spin during our services and concerts. It is a hands-on course in which seven students get to learn how to use turntables and make beats. Our hip-hop/R&B choir, also known as Voices of Redemption (V.O.R.), is for those who have a desire to sing. They learn how to develop their individual voices and sing with a group, learning harmonies and singing different parts. A couple of times a year, the choir leads worship and sings at different outreaches.

Each of these classes has a spiritual emphasis, pointing to Christ as the giver of these gifts. It's always stressed that we should dedicate our talents to him and seek how he wants us to use them. As people go through these groups, we get an indication of where they are spiritually so we can see how and when we can display their talent.

Our drama ministry puts on several major original productions each year that sometimes involve casts of over forty people. These productions feature acting, rapping, singing, dancing, and art. We have several seasoned actors. But for several people, it's their first time, and they soon find a new passion. The stage crew and people building props and painting scenes play a big part as well. A few times a year, we'll also tie in some drama with our message series.

Urban D.: Ay yo my wife is from Queens ■ and I originate from Philly ■ so I've always been a hip-hop fiend ■ (for real) yeah pretty much my whole life

Our media team, Boyz in the Booth, produces several short films that use people from our church as actors. This team also gives camera operators and scriptwriters opportunities to get involved. Plus, some of our church's artists have opened up for nationally known acts when we bring them in for our quarterly concerts. We have monthly open-mic sessions during some of our services, as well as poetry nights called Poet SOUL: Speaking on Urban Life, during which poets and spoken-word artists can share their pieces.

As a result of providing these avenues, we've seen countless people develop their talents to the point where many of them travel across the country sharing their gifts with others as they represent Christ. Each one of these classes, productions, and special events serves as a platform to communicate Christ and gives people a way to use their talents for him.

STRUCTURE

Younger generations despise politics in the church. Several years ago when I was the youth pastor, we were briefly pastorless when one of the pastors left abruptly. A layperson in the church was willing to step up. But a few people weren't sure about him, so others initiated a signature campaign to rally support for him. Some of the young adults got offended by what they perceived to be political activity.

Hip-hoppers in an urban environment don't often discuss government politics. Most don't side with either Democrats or Republicans. They might appreciate that Republicans claim to have values that are more biblical, but many don't feel connected to the Republican Party and have contrary views; for instance, on the U.S. presence in the Middle East. So most people frown on politics as a whole, and most young people feel it doesn't have a place in the church.

> See I knew about Christ ■ but honestly I never really thought twice ■ 'bout committing cause I thought everything that's me I'd be quitting ■ and in a pew in a suit and a tie I'd be sitting (no kidding)

Our church has some good structure in place, but it's practical and not political. By that I mean that we don't have different committees to vote on every little thing, which can easily become a distraction because people get caught up in the internal affairs of the church and forget its real mission. We've developed a system of communication, accountability, and structure that we constantly monitor and make changes to as we continue to grow. Our system isn't perfect, but it works well for our cultural context. Crossover has a church council made up of some of the church staff and some lay members of the church. We meet monthly to make some of the major financial decisions and give councel on spiritual decisions and direction. Our staff meets weekly and makes many day-to-day decisions while overseeing and mentoring the volunteer ministry leaders and workers. Our individual staff members meet monthly with the volunteer ministry leaders who are responsible to them for that particular ministry.

This structure takes much of the pressure off the lead pastor. It empowers the rest of the team, provides for the delegation of responsibility, and causes the church to really have room to grow. People don't have to go to the pastor for approval on every little thing. They know he's available if they need something, but most things they can take up with another staff member. Quarterly, all the ministry leaders and staff get together for a meeting and teaching time. And we have a volunteer training meeting to recast the vision, love on them, and do some general servant training. Once or twice a year, we take our entire leadership and staff on a retreat to spend some time building with each other and having some intimate fellowship.

If you spend any time around hip-hop culture, you know that hip-hoppers tend to buck structure and authority. Several of our staff, including me, wrestled with some of the new structure we implemented a few years ago. We knew we needed it to grow and fulfill God's vision, but like they say, old habits die hard. Attending conferences conducted by some larger innovative churches opened our eyes in many ways. We had to learn to get beyond the mentality of "that's just how I am." If we really wanted to see God do his thing, our crew needed to step it up. I'm proud of my team because we have broken a lot of our cultural stereotypes and have accomplished quite a bit because we've honored God by being more structured. My wife, who was formerly the director of a nonprofit organization, has served in administration the past few years at Crossover and has put some great systems in place. As you model structure, discipline, and organization in your life, you'll see it spread among other leaders and volunteers.

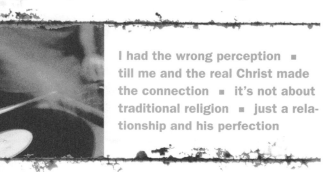

I had the wrong perception ■ till me and the real Christ made the connection ■ it's not about traditional religion ■ just a relationship and his perfection

FINANCES

Can a young urban church impacting hip-hop culture really be self-supporting? Absolutely! Finances will probably always be an issue, but it is possible. People frequently ask me how our church makes it financially, wondering if we are supported from the outside. We thank God for some people who believe in what we are doing and send us some support. But that adds up to less than 5 percent of our annual budget. The vast majority of our budget is raised from within. God has truly done some financial miracles, though we'll never have a budget equal to a suburban church of our size because our crowd is mostly lower to middle working class. But that's okay because we know where we are called. Some suburban people from much higher economic brackets have joined our church, and we praise God for their serving and getting involved, but we know that their segment of the population will never become our primary audience.

When you try to reach a hip-hop audience, finances will be tight, especially in an urban environment. Most of our crowd is in their twenties and thirties. Several are in college, and many work in customer service, restaurants, and retail. But as years pass, we've watched several of our members advance in their careers and a few start their own businesses. There are even a handful of people emerging as young business professionals. I believe that in the years to come, we'll have more people growing in Christ and growing in their education, work ethic, and skills.

Money can be a sensitive thing with younger generations and people in hip-hop culture. Ministries that are big on the prosperity message have given the church a bad name in many urban communities, according to comments I often hear from unchurched people and skeptical people who have visited our church. Put your ear to the street and you'll hear what many hip-hoppers think of the church. They think it's about money, and they view many flashy pastors as fakes or hypocrites. We must be aware of these assumptions and try to tactfully address them. At Crossover, we believe in giving and that God will provide for your needs and bless you if you are faithful to him. But in our weekend services, we don't turn the offering into a big show. We simply share that it's a form of worship and a time when we give back to God a portion of what he has blessed us with. For first-time guests, we thank them for being with us and stress that they don't have to participate. If they want to, they can, but it is a time when our church family gives back to our creator. Occasionally we may briefly share a Scripture. We've had so many comments on how refreshing it is to see the way we handle the offering.

You know what, it's his intention—for you he customized this place ■ with the speakers and the bass ■ so you could feel his grace

There are times when we do share in detail about giving. We do an extensive teaching on giving in our connection classes, and we have discussed it in some of our message series. Our church family has really learned to give. Despite the cultural barriers and being young Christians, many of them have truly found the joy in giving. I believe it comes from education and trust. When we've done a message series on finances, we haven't just focused on giving to the church. These were in-depth messages that taught people to be good stewards in every area of their lives. The Bible has a lot to say about what we should do with the rest of the money that we don't give to God.

When you teach people how to take better care of their overall finances, they can be in a better position to give. Many people for the first time learned how to make a budget and about credit and home ownership. We also regularly hold workshops on these topics. It's important to empower younger adults with this information. When we model and share about giving in a tactful way, we build trust.

And see his face and the others that look just like you ■ he cried for you, he was tried for you

Our ministry also gives an annual ministries and finances report to all of our active members. In our culture of questioning, it clears up any doubts. We openly share the records of all the money that came in and how it was spent. We want our members to know that the leadership is being good stewards and that they can feel confident in how we are using God's money. The report even lists staff salaries so they can see that our team does sacrifice a lot to be there. We're clearly here for the people and not the paycheck. Most of our team have college degrees and could easily make more money elsewhere. But we know this is where God has called us. As the ministry has grown, we have been able to take better care of our staff. But it is still a challenge, since the cost of living and the price of real estate in Florida are skyrocketing.

Look for creative ways to raise funds without constantly taking another offering, which can be a big turnoff. When people come to your worship

And then he died for you and just wants you to be true ■ to him and live and reach the culture ■ and know there's always a spot for you here at Crossover 〞

service, they are most likely going to be there for a couple of hours, including the time they hang out and talk with people. So a creative way to raise money is to sell food. In our hectic world, many people don't grab anything to eat or drink before they come. Selling food creates a great atmosphere and enables people to fellowship longer. Several of our ministries make food and sell it on the patio before and after services. It creates ownership from that ministry as they cook and put everything together. Our building-fund team raises thousands of dollars every year from selling food. Our patio also has a soda machine that even people from the neighborhood frequently use. And our hip-hop shop has a refrigerator with bottled water, Gatorade, and other drinks. Money from the drinks alone helped us buy new equipment, paint, flyers, and other things that would drain the general fund.

When it comes to buying things, our church is very frugal. We get many items at cost or as donations, since we have several people in the church who work in different industries — audio, visual, electrical, home improvement, and flooring. We've learned to make the most of every dollar and do the best we can with what we have. When people see the quality of our leadership team and our campus, given our budget, they are amazed. We've learned how to do a lot with a little. God has always supplied our every need. Finances were extremely rough in the beginning. I was the only staff member and didn't get paid regularly. But as we trusted God, he brought the increase. I never would have imagined we'd be where we are today. It's only with his help. Be encouraged that he will make a way. And as you prove you are faithful with little, he will entrust you with more and more. Remember, our story didn't happen overnight.

11

The Emerging Movement

We got next" is a phrase that's shouted on basketball courts across the planet every day. The ones shouting it are the next team of players ready to jump on the court and get in the game. They're hungry. They're determined. They're energized. This group is almost always convinced they have an idea of how to take the game to the next level and defeat their opponent.

A new movement is emerging, bigger and more important than a basketball game. A global movement filled with young brothers and sisters who have sat on the sidelines and in the bleachers watching the game. Many of them were skeptical and didn't want to be a part of it. Others wanted to participate but found themselves observing from the other side of the fence because they were locked out by the gatekeepers. But the gates have now been left open because of the need for new players. Some jumped at the opportunity, while others were recruited by God's Spirit. They all showed up at practice and began their workouts and spiritual training, moving them from the bleachers to the team bench. They saw all of the action firsthand, the victories and the mistakes. But now the coach is calling them off the bench to jump in the game and make an impact.

Here they are—young, fresh, talented, and full of innovative ideas. They are the next team! Get ready, because the face of the game is about to change.

When you enter a place like Crossover Church—step onto the campus, take in your surroundings, and experience a worship experience—you quickly notice it's not a game. Every detail, from the customization of the facility to every element in the service, has been carefully and prayerfully planned to impact the culture. It's a church like you've never encountered before. It breathes authenticity. The realness emanating from the people, the music, and the speakers is refreshing. You can be yourself and not be judged. There are no cliches, no suits and ties. People are engaging in meaningful conversations and prayer on the patio. You'll also notice that the multicultural crowd is mostly in their twenties, thirties, and forties, though a handful of people are older. You'll notice how on-point things are.

Big Screen

&& These times are pivotal ■ the masses are captured by the digital ■ sucked in by the eye candy, the message is usually subliminal ■ but never minimal

Many people have put in some serious time and energy, using their creativity to make sure things are done with excellence. You might expect some of these organizational aspects from a larger established suburban church, but from a young emerging urban church?

Let me repeat: the face of the church and the way it operates are about to change. If the church is going to survive, they have to!

OTHER MODELS

Crossover may be the first church to fully target hip-hop culture, but many others are now emerging. There is an underground movement of young leaders, pastors, youth pastors, and artists who want to make an impact for Christ. *Newsweek* ran an article on July 31, 2006, about hip-hop in churches that said, "Hip-hop services are popping up all over. Lawndale Community Church in Chicago packs the house for their rap-inspired version. The leaders at Minneapolis's Sanctuary Covenant Church do hip-hop services six times a year to boost youth attendance. Pastor Tommy Kyllonen's Crossover Community Church gained ten times as many congregants when it started using hip-hop."[27] Crossover and several other similar churches have recently been featured in mainstream publications like *USA Today*, the *New York Times*, and the *Philadelphia Inquirer*.

Every November for the past seven years, hundreds of people who want to start similar ministries or transition existing ones to become more effective have gathered at our Fla.vor Fest conference. Several similar conferences have also started in other parts of the country, and several existing conferences have added workshops and separate tracks to train leaders to specifically reach this culture.

Ministries targeting hip-hop culture are popping up all over the map. In 2003, Pastor Phil Jackson started the House, a hip-hop service for youth and young adults in Chicago. What started out as a monthly gathering is developing into its own church that reaches hundreds in its community. That same year, Pastor Efrem Smith started the Sanctuary Covenant Church in Minneapolis. Although hip-hop culture is not his main target, they have hip-hop Sundays every six weeks and have a hip-hop academy in which they teach the arts. Meeting at a local high school, they have seen incredible growth as their multicultural congregation has grown to over seven hundred. Pastor Phil and Pastor Efrem also wrote an amazing book together titled *The Hip-Hop Church*, in which they especially focus on the African-American church's struggle with hip-hop. The book brings a solid perspective from both sides and presents hope that the urban church really can engage the culture.

Examples of other hip-hop ministries are Extraordinary Young People, a ministry that works specifically with Native American youth on reservations. Hip-hop has become huge on Indian reservations. Our team works closely with their staff as they model their youth churches after Crossover. Their organization plans to plant ten hip-hop-style churches on reservations by 2010. Early in 2005, Pastor Lee Wilson, an urban youth-ministry veteran with close to twenty years of experience, planted Generation Church in Atlanta, targeting hip-hoppers under forty. Our ministry receives several emails each month from new ministries launching in places like Colorado, Kentucky, California, and South Florida. Some of them have visited us or attended our conference. Several of them we've never met, yet they thank us for our model and our resources. We've even received several emails from Australia, Africa, and Europe, where ministries are engaging hip-hop culture and keeping up with us through our website.

Several artists are stepping up to lead ministries as well. Fros'T is a hip-hop artist who has been doing urban youth ministry at his church in Los Angeles for years. In 2006, he took the pastoral position at Victory Outreach Chapel. William Branch, aka the Ambassador, from the Cross Movement, graduated from Dallas Theological Seminary in 2004 and currently co-pastors Epiphany Fellowship, a new church plant in North Philly. After praying and studying church planting for years, DJ Rhino planted a church targeting hip-hop culture in Gary, Indiana. Even hip-hop veteran Kurtis Blow has started a Thursday night hip-hop service, partnering with Greater Hood Memorial AME Church in Harlem. Each one of these ministries has its own flavor and personality, but these emerging leaders are already making a huge impact in their cities.

There is also a group of older established ministers who saw the need and started separate hip-hop-style services to reach the younger generations. Isaias Rivera pastors a church just outside of Boston that was declining until about a year ago. They did some monthly outreaches using hip-hop, led by young adults in the church. They saw hundreds of people attend, and God began to stir this fifty-year-old pastor's heart. It definitely wasn't his style, but he saw the impact. Around that same time, he saw an article on Pastors.com about our ministry. He was going to be in Florida on vacation with his family just two weeks later. He visited a service, and we talked afterward on the patio. When he returned home, he told his board that he knew God was calling the church to begin a major shift. Some of them thought he was crazy, but others were fully supportive.

Pastor Isaias brought some of his leaders to our conference a few months later and also brought a hip-hop choreographer named Wilson, who wasn't a Christian but attended their outreaches. I recently heard the incredible story of how he accepted Christ during the Friday night concert at the conference. When he went back to the hotel, he couldn't stop talking about it. And that weekend he

> The way they pimp the propaganda is criminal ▪ they push they views on the culture ▪ as they lounging on the sofa

gave a testimony in their church. Their congregation and the people in the community were astonished that Wilson now followed Christ. It was a real turning point in their ministry. An influential person in their community had accepted Christ and was now passionate about it! Since then, they have transitioned their worship style, programs, and messages to focus on people influenced by hip-hop. More visitors now attend from the community, and the church is growing and continuing to see lives changed.

Dr. Derek Guyten is a fifty-seven-year-old African-American senior pastor at First Missionary Baptist Church in Marin City, California. When Pastor Guyten started leading his current church, he had just under a hundred members with a median age of sixty and no youth attending. He quickly realized that none of the churches in his community were reaching the younger urban culture. He visited the Holy Hip-Hop Awards in Atlanta and was greatly moved. He studied hip-hop culture and the postmodern generation and became more excited about engaging in this type of ministry. About five years ago, he did some outreach concerts that eventually turned into a Saturday night hip-hop outreach service. Soon, about one hundred younger people attended; about 60 percent of them didn't have any church background. The first year, close to fifty accepted Christ, and many eventually attended their Sunday service plus their midweek Bible study. Pastor Guyten attributed this to the post-

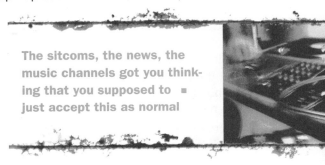

The sitcoms, the news, the music channels got you thinking that you supposed to just accept this as normal

modern value that being authentic is more important than being relative.

The churches in his area were indifferent but polite as they tried to stay in the middle of the road with their opinions. After doing some workshops with local ministries, he realized the huge need for educating church leaders on this subject. He recently finished his doctorate and wrote a thesis titled "Engaging the Congregation in an Intergenerational Hip-Hop Outreach Ministry at First Missionary Baptist in Marin City, California." Pastor Guyten recently put together a booklet about using hip-hop as an outreach ministry with DVDs and sample video clips. God has opened doors for him to train leaders nationally and overseas. I'm excited to see pastors of the gatekeepers' generation engaging hip-hop culture and helping bridge the gap with pastors and leaders in their age group.

REACHING BEYOND THE TARGET AUDIENCE

In 2002, we felt God was calling our ministry to target hip-hop culture. Naively, we assumed that would box us into a very young but large demographic. Although our congregation is younger than most, it has been amazing to watch what else God has done. Many older parents visited as a result of their teenager or twentysomething being drawn to our church. Soon, we saw several of them become members and get involved. Some of these parents had never even been in church before, while others were burned out from traditional churches and were looking for something more real and fresh. They loved what was happening, believed in the vision, and wanted to be a part of it. They saw not only how it was affecting their children but how God was working in their own lives.

God has sent us some great leaders and mentors who were looking for the right place to serve and be used. Israel and Sylvia Cabrera had previously been in ministry at a couple of churches but eventually got burned out and found themselves just church attenders for several years. They both knew that God wanted them to give back. Their children were in their late teens and early twenties and weren't really happy at the church the family attended. Their kids soon started attending our church. Israel and Sylvia decided to visit and check out this "hip-hop church." At first, they were a little skeptical. But once they attended a service, felt God's love, and met the people, they soon began to ask God if this was where they were supposed to be as an entire family. Soon they felt the green light and became members.

My wife and I built a relationship with Israel and Sylvia, and they expressed that they'd love to serve in some way but didn't know where. Our congregation was growing with many young married couples, and we saw a huge need for some type of marriage ministry. Israel and Sylvia were an awesome couple, married over twenty-five years and with some real wisdom to share. Although they were in their late forties, they were Hispanics from the Northeast and were able to relate to hip-hoppers even though they were not hip-hoppers themselves. They have been such an incredible blessing to our ministry, counseling countless couples and leading special events attended by up to sixty couples. They also lead two separate small groups for married couples at their home, and they are always packed.

> A few years back, who would have ever thought same-sex marriage would be official and formal ∎ I'm not here to be cordial

Although the majority of our audience is into hip-hop, people who aren't are still welcomed and aren't made to feel like outcasts. Hip-hop is now mainstream pop music, so it is not some foreign thing. We even have younger individuals who aren't into hip-hop who have joined our church. They love the realness, the vibe, and being able to come to a place where people don't judge their appearance. We have some twentysomething members who are in a punk rock band and live together in a community. I performed a wedding ceremony for a couple from their crew recently. They definitely look a lot different with their several piercings, tattoos, and dreadlocks. But they are welcomed, loved, aren't judged, and have a place to connect and serve.

Some retirees in their sixties have joined our church in the past few years. One woman told me that she originally came to bring her grand-kids. But she found herself being fed and growing more than she ever had before. Another sixty-one-year-old grandmother approached me tearfully on the patio and shared that although she had been in church for over twenty years, God had spoken to her the most at our church. I was humbled and in tears myself hearing these types of comments.

I vividly remember a Thursday night in the spring of 2003. Al and Gail Alonzo, along with their daughter, who was in her midtwenties, walked onto the patio to visit the youth service. I immediately noticed Al and Gail, since they looked much older than the rest of the crowd. I greeted them, wondering what they would think of us, since we were doing a panel discussion about sex in our youth service that evening! After the service, they ap-

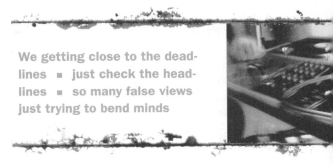

We getting close to the dead-lines ■ just check the head-lines ■ so many false views just trying to bend minds

proached me, hugged me, and let me know they loved it. They said that they had found their church. From then on, they regularly attended every single service.

That summer, their family attended our membership class, and at the end of the class, Al and Gail pulled my wife, Lucy, aside for prayer. Al was sixty-two years old, and for the first time in his life, he prayed a prayer to accept Christ. Here was someone older than my parents being led to Christ for the very first time at a hip-hop-style church. I was blown away by what God can do! Al had been an alcoholic his whole life and had had four strokes. Gail had been a believer, but Al would never commit to God or go to church regularly. I had the privilege of renewing Al and Gail's wedding vows after forty years of marriage.

Al and Gail have been such a giving couple, and they now lead our public access television ministry. Each week, they volunteer countless hours of editing services for the program and fulfilling orders for DVDs of our services.

We value our older members, include them, and give them a place to serve. Even though you may have a target audience, you can still reach well beyond it and have a multigenerational church.

NOW WHAT?

I know there will be a diverse group of people reading this book: church leaders, pastors, youth pastors, church volunteers, concerned parents, artists, and fans of the music. Now that you have read the book this far, you might be wondering, "How do I process all of this and take action in my church, my community, and maybe even in my own home? Where do I start?" Here are some thoughts on that for church leaders, parents, and hip-hoppers.

To Church Leaders

For church leaders, staff, and volunteers, I'd challenge you to pray about what God is doing in your heart. You obviously have a desire to reach younger generations and to see the Great Commission fulfilled. We want to see the world changed. I pray that these words have given you inspiration and hope. God gives each ministry a unique vision for its community. Our vision and the methods we use to carry it out will be different and diverse. Maybe you picked up this book because you are curious about hip-hop and its implications in your area. You may not have realized how wide its influence is. Or maybe you do realize hip-hop's influence, but you need more resources to help you reach those who are being influenced. Either way, you see the need, and it's time for some action.

We as leaders must be willing to change, even if that's not our preference. We can't get too comfortable. We live in an ever-changing culture, so we must find new ways to present the never-changing message of Christ. Don't settle. If your ministry has settled, I encourage you to find ways to get it stirred up and moving forward again. I can't stress enough that we must be students of the culture. I encourage you to read and to read some more. If you want to get updated on the world of hip-hop, there is a wealth of books, magazines, and websites you can regularly check out. (See the resources section of this book.) By staying up on these things, you'll easily be able to tie current events into message illustrations and one-on-one conversations. Even if you're not part of the culture, those people who are in it will feel more connected to you when you're talking about things that are familiar to them. This book is a first step in your learning. I encourage you to attend some conferences and training events where you can take more steps and build relationships with others who have the same desire.

The intention of hip-hop is to express how you see life. Of course, we see a lot of immorality in hip-hop, but that's how the artists see life. There are now opportunities all over the world for individual believers and the church to express how we see life. Ask God what he's calling your ministry to do. I encourage you to continue the conversation. Gather some youth and young adults and get some feedback. Hear their heart, passion, and ideas to reach their peers. Plan on taking some action, whether it's an outreach, a concert, a new service, or partnering with another church. The possibilities are endless. Get creative and use your young adults and youth to spearhead the initiative. I look forward to hearing your story!

To Parents

The fact that you're reading this book shows your sincere concern for your kids. They may be younger children, teens, or even young adults. Please be aware of the cultures that influence your children. Don't be ignorant or naive. I meet parents all the time who buy their kids secular hip-hop CDs full of profanity and a twisted worldview. Many of these parents are clueless about the CDs' content, while others just blow it off. This definitely influences your kids' attitude, language, and spirituality. Be proactive and get involved in your kids' interests. I encourage you to monitor what your kids are listening to, what they're watching, and what websites they visit. More tough love is needed, including taking some of their stuff away. I advocate that you take inappropriate music away, but replace it. Dozens of quality Christ-centered hip-hop albums come out in

> So I'm presenting the facts ■ we gotta get back to the basics like the book of Acts ■ you ever seen the maps ■ and to the extent they spread it

stores each year. Even more come out on the internet. It may be a good idea to have a youth pastor or young adult in the church introduce the new music to your kids and get them familiar with the Christian artists. Most cities regularly have Christian hip-hop artists come to different events. Take your kids to some of these events and have them see someone from the culture who serves God and is not ashamed to represent him.

Though I encourage you to be proactive and get involved in your kids' interests, you should still be yourself. If you didn't grow up on hip-hop, please don't try to use hip-hop slang or dress like your kids. I've seen some parents try to play the part, and it was ridiculous. They need you to be their parent, not one of their homies (peers). But continue to learn about their world so God can help you bridge those gaps as you parent and guide them.

Each night, I go into my daughters' bedrooms after they're asleep and pray for them. They look so sweet and innocent as they sleep, but they're living in a sinful world that influences them, even at their young ages, to go in the wrong direction. We must cover our kids with prayer every day.

To My Fellow Hip-Hoppers

I guess I'll be the hardest on my fellow hip-hoppers, because the torch is being passed to you. The time has come for us to really step it up. Yes, the music in the Christian hip-hop community has stepped up: our quality, beats, lyrics, album covers, concerts, and stage presence. Much of what we do definitely competes with mainstream. I meet so many people making some incredible art for Christ with next to nothing. It's the true essence of underground hip-hop. I'd argue that many Christ-centered hip-hop artists have more talent than most hip-hop artists today. We've stepped it up in many ways, but what about our personal walk with God?

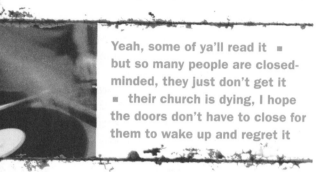

Yeah, some of ya'll read it ■ but so many people are closed-minded, they just don't get it ■ their church is dying, I hope the doors don't have to close for them to wake up and regret it

Are we concentrating our efforts on personal devotion time, studies, accountability, and daily witness, foundational areas that are more important than the outward stuff that others see? It can't be just about listening to the music or making the music or rocking a crowd. The music and the movement are edifying, but what are we really doing with it after the show or after we turn off our iPods?

Being part of hip-hop culture and ministering to it can be a fine line to walk. So let's be real. Some of you reading this are hip-hop, meaning you grew up in the culture and probably were engulfed by the negative aspects at one time. When we don't have safeguards and don't have solid people to whom we are accountable, those old things can creep back into our lives. For some people, they never left in the first place. Many of us find ourselves carrying this baggage on our Christian journey. One of those scary things in our old suitcase is the mentality that I'm the dopest, I'm the best, I'm the flyest. Unfortunately, some of that exists in Christian hip-hop today. Didn't the apostle Paul say that it was only in Christ that he would boast?

Another item in the suitcase is the desire to be famous or go platinum. Of course, it's all for Christ—or is it? The desire to be the center of attention has also leaked into the Christian hip-hop community. Sad to say, I've met several people like this. When the disciples got too much limelight, didn't they play it down and quickly point to Christ? The other flashy item in the old suitcase is having the latest things to impress others. We've seen a lot of that too. In Galatians 1:10, Paul asks, "Am I now trying to win human approval, or God's approval? Or am I trying to please people? If I were still trying to please people, I would not be a servant of Christ." Too many people want that human approval.

When I address these mentalities, I'm focusing not only on us as individuals but also on us as a movement of people ministering to hip-hop culture. When we look at all this baggage that still pops up, it pushes me to ask the question, What are we buying into? Are we buying what culture is selling us, or what Scripture is instructing us? Think hard about that. I challenge you to ask yourself how you spend your time, energy, and money. That will tell you where your heart is. We must be accountable. We all make mistakes, struggle, and doubt. But we need someone to share this with, someone to vent to, and someone to push us and encourage us to stay on track. James 5:16 says, "Therefore confess your sins to each other and pray for each other so that you may be healed. The prayer of a righteous person is powerful and effective." We all need to be healed of some stuff. We need accountability partners and mentors to push us through our junk.

The Christian hip-hop community needs to take it beyond the concerts and the CDs we produce. Those are great evangelism tools, and they help edify the believer as well. But then what? What happens to the young person who accepts Christ at the concert? We need to become a proactive part of discipleship in a local church. The church needs you! I continually meet several artists and fans of the music who have little or no connection to a church in their own city. You are a vital part in bridging the gap, because you understand the culture first-hand. You are the one who can continue the discussion and create the action plan with your pastors and church leaders after they read this book. Find a place you can serve. Maybe it's in an existing ministry, or maybe God is calling you to start something brand new. Every day, the baton is being passed to the younger generation. Let's not drop it!

The state of the planet is so pathetic ■ so many say it's too hard, just forget it ■ we look for deals like Expedia ■ but we can ignore the world as it gets greedier

THE FUTURE OF THE EMERGING CHURCH

In the United States, we can look at all the trends and see the white church declining while the immigrant church, the African-American church, the Spanish-speaking church, and the multicultural church grow by leaps and bounds. Within a decade or so, most metropolitan areas in the U.S. will see more nonwhite Christians than white. It seems like a paradox that most of the leadership in mainstream Christianity is still white. Even the face of the emerging church is mostly white. At emerging-church conferences, there may be twenty-five speakers and only one or two are nonwhite. The emerging church is not just the twenty-seven-year-old blond male with a patch of hair under his bottom lip. The emerging church is also the young black male in the hood. It is the second-generation Mexican in LA and the child of Chinese immigrants in Houston. The emerging church is the Puerto Rican female on Wall Street. This paints a more accurate picture of the emerging church. The church as a whole must train more ethnic leaders and train nonethnic leaders to better lead in these settings that are quickly becoming the majority.

Communities of faith will continue to take on new shapes. Authenticity and realness will grow. Relationships will become more important as people's overall number of relationships will decrease. Technology's role in the church will continue to increase. Podcasts, streaming music, information, and communication will rely more on the internet. Worship experiences will become more visual as new technology is developed and leaders realize they need to better engage people's visual senses. The arts, like film, poetry, and dance, will play a greater role as people's passions and talents are given a greater platform to express their faith. As churches are pressed to find bigger facilities in metropolitan areas, more will instead branch out with video venues, since younger people are accustomed to watching the big screen. These are church venues that have live worship, but the message is on the big screen from the main campus. This will be a fine line to walk, as people will want interaction more than ever. The campus pastors and leaders in these venues will need to get creative and mix in some live teaching among other elements in order to develop and keep a real community. Hip-hop and other popular music genres will become more accepted and used in worship as well as in the overall culture of these emerging faith communities.

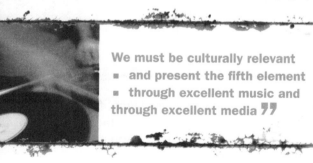

We must be culturally relevant

- and present the fifth element
- through excellent music and through excellent media 🙶

It's encouraging to watch transformation take place as many churches are truly engaging the culture and people are building relationships with Christ for the first time. I'm excited. I'm hopeful. I know God is working!

Sunday Programming Sheet

FIRST SERVICE, 10:00 A.M.

TIME	ELEMENT	PEOPLE	SOUND	LIGHTING	VIDEO	NOTES
9:30	Prayer	Team		Everything up		
9:45	Doors open	Hospitality team	DJ plays music	Everything up	Announcement screens	Countdown screens start at 10 minutes (9:50)
10:00	Opening prayer	Josie	Wireless mic	Stage lit, house dim	Cameras	Keep light boxes on side walls illuminated
10:02	Worship	Harmony (worship team), artist, and poets	Mics, DJ, and instruments	Stage lit, house dim	Cameras with worship words displayed over	Poetry and Scripture reading mixed in while artist airbrushes a mural
10:25	Prayer/greeting	Derrick	Wireless, DJ	Everything up	Cameras	DJ spins music
10:27	Announcements	Lucy	Wireless mic, DJ	Everything up	Announcement screens	Close curtains, DJ spins an instrumental backdrop
10:30	Offering	Carl	Wireless mic, CD track	Everything up	Cameras	Play Ambassador "Body Talk" from the Thesis
10:34	Video message intro.			Everything off		

182

Time	Element	Person	Mic	Lighting	Camera	Screens/Stage
10:35	Message: "Sexploitation"	Tommy	Earpiece	Everything up	Cameras and motion slides	Drama set is prepared behind the curtains
10:55	Drama	Team	Lapel mics	Stage lit, house dim	Cameras	Curtains open
10:58	Message with Q&A and testimonies	Tommy and panel of single and married people	Earpiece and wireless mics	Everything up	Cameras and motion slides	Back screens display "Sexploitation" artwork
11:12	Song: "I'm Not Everyone"	Los 1	Wireless mic	Stage lit, house dim	Cameras	Back screens play video footage from song
11:17	Closing prayer and dismissal	Tone	Wireless mic	Stage lit, house dim	Cameras	Back screens display next week's title and artwork

SECOND SERVICE, 11:45 A.M. (SAME FORMAT)

THIRD SERVICE, 7:00 P.M. (ADD A SET FOR A GUEST HIP-HOP ARTIST)

183

Sample Topics for Message Series

Here are some message series that Crossover Community Church has used in the past few years. We use both topical and expository teaching, many times blending the two. Our series generally run three to six weeks. Every message is intended to shape a Christ-centered world-view and to give a challenge that includes practical application. Many times there is an opportunity for people to start a relationship with Christ.

- "Reasonable Doubt." A four-week series that looked into the historical evidence that the Bible is accurate and that Christ really did live, die, and resurrect. The series included interviews from a local urban flea market.
- "MySpace: Is God Invited?" A four-week series focusing on identity, community, time, and space. We tied in original short films and used the MySpace network as a theme.
- "The Church Should ..." A longer series that went through the book of 1 Corinthians, looking at many of the struggles the early church went through and how many in a faith community still struggle with those issues today.
- "Sexploitation: The Truth about Sexuality and Relationships." A five-week series that looked at sex from a biblical view for those who are single, dating, and married. The series included drama, panel discussions, and testimonies.
- "Sex in the Church?" A four-week series taking a candid look at lust. Pornography, premarital sex, adultery, homosexuality, and masturbation were all hot topics that we tackled from a biblical perspective.
- "City of Pain." So many experience anger, deceit, confusion, and shattered dreams, and they don't know what to do with the hurt. The series climaxed with a message of forgiveness and moving on.
- "The Spirituality in Hip-Hop." This four-week series shared some hip-hop history and biblical history and touched on contradiction, materialism, and living in the culture while finding balance. Each week was accompanied by a continuing short film.

"The Search for Purpose." This six-week series was adapted from Rick Warren's Forty Days of Purpose Campaign. Each title was changed to a question, and we tweaked the content a bit, illustrating it with many things from our culture.

"Extreme Makeover Series: Discovering True Happiness beneath the Surface." A four-week series using short films and messages based on popular makeover shows: Rig My Ride, Crossover Cribs, The Apprentice's, and Cut and Cover. Even if you have a new car, a new house, a new job, a new body, without Christ you'll still be empty.

"Wake Up!" A five-week series from the book of Malachi that looked at how the Israelite culture was so similar to ours today, highlighting false sacrifices, corrupt leaders, unfaithfulness, and judgment.

"The Creator's Top 10." A six-week series counting down the Ten Commandments from ten to number one. It was formatted as a video-countdown show with hosts and a song that accompanied the message.

"The Sales Pitch: What Are You Buying Into?" This five-week series looked at the many ways the world tries to get our attention: walk-up pitch, commercials, pop-up ads, junk mail, and identity theft. It challenged the worldview we buy into.

"Crossover: Play by HIS Rules." A three-week series with a basketball theme based on a movie that deals with authority. We looked at earthly authority and ultimately God's authority.

"Let's Get Up: Do My Prayers Matter?" A five-week series that asked hard questions about prayer and its effects. These messages also walked people through the Lord's Prayer and broke down the words behind it.

"Heaven: Our Final Destination?" Most people want to go to heaven, but even Christians can't tell you much about it. This five-week series smashed many myths and focused on what we do know about heaven from the Scriptures.

"The Hustle." A six-week series from the book of Ecclesiastes. These messages focused on materialism and our personal drives and agendas. It included poetry and hip-hop songs that paraphrased King Solomon's words.

Resources

BOOKS

Ashley, Jennifer, ed. *Relevant Church*. Orlando: Relevant, 2004.

Chang, Jeff. *Can't Stop, Won't Stop: A History of the Hip-Hop Generation*. New York: St. Martin's, 2005.

Darby, Derrick, and Tommie Shelby. *Hip-Hop and Philosophy: Rhyme 2 Reason*. Chicago: Open Court, 2005.

Detweiler, Craig, and Barry Taylor. *Matrix of Meaning: Finding God in Pop Culture*. Grand Rapids, MI: Baker, 2003.

Gee, Alex, and John Teter. *Jesus and the Hip-Hop Prophets: Spiritual Insights from Lauryn Hill and Tupac Shakur*. Downers Grove, IL: InterVarsity, 2003.

George, Nelson. *Hip-Hop America*. New York: Penguin, 2005.

Kitwanan, Bakari. *The Hip-Hop Generation: Young Blacks and the Crisis in African American Culture*. New York: Basic Civitas Books, 2002.

———. *Why White Kids Love Hip-Hop: Wankstas, Wiggas, Wannabes, and the New Reality of Race in America*. New York: Basic Civitas Books, 2005.

Pinn, Anthony, ed. *Noise and Spirit: The Religious and Spiritual Sensibilities of Rap Music*. New York: New York Univ. Press, 2003.

Simmons, Russell. *Life and Def: Sex, Drugs, Money, and God*. With Nelson George. New York: Crown, 2001.

Smith, Efrem, and Phil Jackson. *The Hip-Hop Church*. Downers Grove, IL: InterVarsity, 2005.

Zydek, Heather, ed. *Relevant Nation*. Orlando: Relevant, 2006.

MAGAZINES

Secular

Elemental (elementalmag.com)
The Source (thesource.com)
Vibe (vibe.com)
XXL (xxlmag.com)

Christian

Relevant (relevantmagazine.com). Has some hip-hop.
SOUL Mag (flavoralliance.com)

DOCUMENTARY MOVIES ON HIP-HOP

The Freshest Kids (2002). A history of the B-boy (break dancing).
The MC (2005). Why we do it (about rappers).
Scratch (2002). DJ documentary.
Style Wars (1983). A history of graffiti.

WEBSITES

www.christianhiphopper.com
www.dasouth.com
www.gospelflava.com
www.holyhiphop.com
www.reachlife.org
www.sphereofhiphop.com
www.theambassadoronline.com
www.theyuinon.com
www.urbangospelalliance.com
www.urbnet.org
www.whyhiphop.com
www.wtwmagazine.com

RECORD LABELS

www.beatmart.com
www.crossmovement.com
www.flavoralliance.com
www.gotee.com
www.lampmode.com
www.reachrecords.com

ONLINE RADIO

www.altaredlives.org
www.holycultureradio.com

EVENTS TO HELP YOU REACH HIP-HOP CULTURE

Fla.vor Fest (www.flavoralliance.com). Held annually the first weekend of November, Fla.vor Fest is a four-day conference at Crossover Community Church in Tampa. Fla.vor Fest Summit is a two-day event held in select cities at churches targeting the culture.

Reload (www.reloadtour.org). Held in more than twenty cities throughout the year, Reload features a one-day training experience at a great price and with great speakers.
Urban Youth Workers Institute Conference (www.uywi.org). A three-day conference held annually in May at Azusa Pacific University. This is the largest gathering of urban leaders in the country.

NATIONAL HIP-HOP EVENTS

Fla.vor Fest (www.flavoralliance.com). This conference in Tampa features church services, twenty-four workshops in multiple tracks, and forty-eight artists on two stages. Held annually the first weekend of November.
Holy Hip-Hop Awards (www.holyhiphop.com). Held every January, this two-day event in Atlanta includes showcases, workshops, fellowship, and an awards ceremony.
Rap Fest (www.rapfest2000.com). This outreach-oriented event in the Bronx features eight hours of Christian hip-hop in the park. Held every August.

HIP-HOP BIBLES AND DEVOTIONALS

Elementz of Life (www.elementzoflife.com). Devotional from American Bible Society. Includes devotionals, stories, testimonies, poetry, pictures, and artwork. The program also features an evangelistic CD.
The Epic (www.gettheepic.com). A hip-hop version of the Gospel of John by Fred Lynch.
Real (www.thomasnelson.com). A hip-hop-influenced Biblezine published by Thomas Nelson.

CHURCHES THAT TARGET HIP-HOP CULTURE

www.crossoverchurch.org
www.sanctuarycovenant.org
www.thahouse.org
www.youthexplosion.com

Credits

Lyrics from the following songs are quoted in the chapters of this book by permission of Urban D.:

Chapter 1: "Roots Chapter 3" from the album *The Tranzlation*. © 2001 by Urban D.

Chapter 2: "Skintone" from the album *The Missin' Element*. © 1999 by Urban D.

Chapter 3: "The Value" from the album *The Immigrant V. 2*. © 2004 by Urban D.

Chapter 4: "Wait" from the album *The Immigrant V. 2*. © 2004 by Urban D.

Chapter 5: "Hip-Hop" from the album *Un.orthodox*. © 2007 by Urban D.

Chapter 6: "Hip-Hop" from the album *Un.orthodox*. © 2007 by Urban D.

Chapter 7: "Hip-Hop" from the album *Un.orthodox*. © 2007 by Urban D.

Chapter 8: "American Dream" from the album *The Immigrant V. 2*. © 2004 by Urban D.

Chapter 9: "What We Do Now" from the album *The Tranzlation*. © 2001 by Urban D.

Chapter 10: "Crossover," featuring Rize, from Rize's album *Hardheaded*. © 2004 by Urban D.

Chapter 11: "Big Screen" from the Fla.vor Alliance self-titled album. © 2005 by Urban D.

Notes

1. Robert Caro, *The Power Broker* (New York: Knopf, 1974), 840–41.

2. "Rockefeller Drug Laws: Perpetuating Institutional Racism," http://www.drugpolicy.org/statebystate/newyork/rockhistory/, accessed December 11, 2006.

3. Peter Hamill, "The Gangs," *New York Post*, May 1972.

4. Jeff Chang, *Can't Stop, Won't Stop* (New York: St. Martin's, 2005), 117.

5. Ibid., 106.

6. Personal interview via email.

7. Russell Simmons, *Life and Def* (New York: Crown, 2001), 61.

8. http://www.80sreborn.com/rap.shtml.

9. Harry Allen, "Public Enemy: Leading a Radio Rebellion," *Black Renaissance Exclusive*, February 26, 1988, 9–10.

10. Paul Grein, "Popeye: Rappers Welcome MTV's Enthusiasm," *Los Angeles Times*, June 18, 1989.

11. James Haskins, *One Nation under a Groove: Rap Music and Its Roots* (New York: Hyperion, 2000), 103.

12. Janice Kelly, "The Printed Word," *Advertising Age*, May 11, 1992, 45.

13. Ben Bagdikian, *The Media Monopoly* (Boston: Beacon, 1997), xiii.

14. Chang, *Can't Stop, Won't Stop*, 443.

15. Julie Watson, "Rapper's Delight: A Billion Dollar Industry," Forbes.com, February 18, 2004, http://www.forbes.com/entrepreneurs/2004/02/18/cx_jw_0218 hiphop.html.

16. Ibid.

17. *USA Today*, February 6, 2006.

18. Ibid.

19. Ibid.

20. Barna Group, "Most Twentysomethings Put Christianity on the Shelf Following Spiritually Active Teen Years," *Barna Update*, September 11, 2006, http://www.barna .org/FlexPage.aspx?Page=BarnaUpdate&BarnaUpdateID=245, accessed December 11, 2006.

21. "Postmodernism," in *The Columbia Encyclopedia*, 6th ed. (New York: Columbia Univ. Press, 2006).

22. Derrick Darby and Tommie Shelby, *Hip-Hop and Philosophy: Rhyme 2 Reason* (Chicago: Open Court, 2005), 209–10.

23. "Oversight: Film Piracy in New York City," June 29, 2006, nyccouncil.info.

24. familysafemedia.com.

25. Barna Group, "Survey Shows How Christians Share Their Faith," *Barna Update*, January 31, 2005, http://www.barna.org/FlexPage.aspx?Page=BarnaUpdate &BarnaUpdateID=181, accessed December 11, 2006.

26. Dan Kimball, *The Emerging Church* (Grand Rapids, MI: Zondervan, 2003), 136.

27. Lilit Marcus and Patton Dodd, "Beliefwatch: 'Word,' " *Newsweek*, July 31, 2006, http://www.msnbc.msn.com/id/13989904/site/newsweek/.

CROSSOVER RESOURCES

S.O.U.L MAG

S.O.U.L.MAG (Speaking On Urban Life)

This new magazine brings together the former Crossover and Fla.vor Fest magazines. Released twice a year (spring and fall), the magazine continues to focus on Crossover Church and Fla.vor Fest but offers even more content with thought-provoking articles on faith and culture. There are lots of great ads and even music and resource reviews too. Available exclusively through our website.

Press Play series I and II

These DVDs are collections of short films created for message series at Crossover. These films can be used for personal enjoyment, in small group settings, or in large worship gatherings. The DVDs also include a Crossover worship experience, commercials, intros, and music videos. If you are a pastor, youth pastor, or leader and you've been looking for a way to visually engage people as you speak to them, these DVDs are excellent tools.

Message Series

These message series, which have been used at Crossover, are relevant to urban and hip-hop culture. Topics include: "MySpace ... Is God Invited?" "The Sales Pitch," "Spirituality in Hip-Hop," "Extreme Makeovers," and more. For each series, you can download transcripts, outlines, and PowerPoint presentations, add your own flavor, and then teach it in your ministry. Video clips from the Press Play DVDs can be used with these series.

Harmony "Crossover's Worship Team"

Harmony has definitely stepped it up to a new level on this double disc of worship songs and instrumentals. Not only can you enjoy playing the worship songs on disc 1 on your stereo, but you can also use the instrumental versions of these songs on disc 2 as a soundtrack for your church to sing with during your worship services.

Fla.vor Fest DVD Series

These DVDs feature footage from the annual Hip-Hop/Emerging Ministries Conference held at Crossover Church in Tampa, Florida. Crossover has become an international model as a church that solely targets people who are influenced by hip-hop culture. Thousands have come from all over the world to attend Fla.vor Fest and experience the new face of the emerging urban church through workshops, services, fellowship, and the dope evening festival concerts. These DVDs highlight the hottest performances and include bonus footage of workshops and services, artist interviews, and music videos.

Crossover Service DVD's

Now you can check out a Crossover worship experience at home or show it to your people. These DVDs include the worship service and teaching, showing all of the unique elements of many of Crossover's services. Series include "Sexploitation," "The Creator's Top Ten," "Ghetto," "Reasonable Doubt," and more.